How To Improve Your Speculative Fiction Openings

2nd edition

Robert Qualkinbush

ReAnimus Press

Breathing Life into Great Books

ReAnimus Press
1100 Johnson Road #16-143
Golden, CO 80402
www.ReAnimus.com

Special thanks to the Theodore Sturgeon Literary Trust for permission to quote extensively from "Cactus Dance" and "The Man Who Figured Everything."

ISBN-13: 978-1490555270

Second print edition: July, 2013

10 9 8 7 6 5 4 3 2 1

TABLE OF CONTENTS

FOREWORD

This is a landmark piece of work. New writers are always looking for *The Secret* to becoming a professional author. It's extremely rare to find actual shards of any such Secret—many claim there is no such thing—but here is one.

The analysis Robert has done here is hard research. He's dug through a lot of stories from pros and hopeful authors and found something previously unknown in the openings of those stories that uniquely separates the pros from the mass of unpublished authors.

When I founded the Critters Writers' Workshop it was because there was no other writers workshop on the web. I was hopeful that by harnessing the power of all the writers out there we could all help each other improve and lift up every aspiring author into a pro who could possibly become one. Critters has had nearly 30,000 writers join since then, many of them starting from scratch and turning into award-caliber professionals. This has provided a rich universe of data to mine—which Robert has done.

Robert has analyzed the openings of over 1,400(!) speculative fiction pieces—science fiction, fantasy, and some horror—from both professionals and new writers and found a slice of that long-sought-after Secret to what makes pro selling stories work. As the title says, this book is filled with tons of examples that show you how to improve your openings so they'll help you sell your story.

If you want to be a professional writer, you have to read this piece. Following the advice and examples herein is not a guarantee of selling to pro markets, of course. You still have to do everything else that makes a compelling story with beloved characters, but your story openings are your doorway to sales—either open or closed. Many otherwise salable stories may well have never been read by editors or first readers simply because they never got past the opening.

I love it when someone applies the principles of scientific analyses to learn new truths, so it's with great pleasure that I present to you a critical shard of *The Secret*. Use it well, and get those tales published.

—Dr. Andrew Burt
Founder,
Critters Writers' Workshop
www.Critique.org

INTRODUCTION

Not long ago I read a short story in *The New Yorker* written in first-person point of view. Cues from the narrator led both my wife and I to assume that said narrator was female. We found out, many pages into it, that the narrator was supposed to be male. As a reader, I was forced to back-pedal and mentally revise what I'd thought was going on.

As a reader, my "dream state" was shattered, and I felt annoyance at the author. This problem, forcing the reader to mentally back-pedal, is a major peril for beginning speculative fiction writers. It's a fairly common experience to start reading a beginners' story, and after the first scene has gone on for pages, to suddenly realize that the POV character is a sentient bee, an angel, or a were-dragon. The author knew this, but didn't convey it until far too late, and the mental images and assumptions you'd developed as a reader had to be scrapped. You've probably had this experience, if you've read many beginners' stories.

I hope this book will help you to steer between the reefs of infodumps on the one side, and on the other, forcing the reader to back-pedal because of a poorly "set-up" first scene. It often only takes a sentence or two to set-up your first scene. But those few sentences are critical. This book will, I hope, give you some tools and strategies to figure out what needs to "lead" in your story, and what can be laced in later, so that your reader has a smooth and enjoyable reading experience. Your better SF & F writers have the ability to create a planned ambiguity—to anticipate the cognitive assumptions a reader will make—to draw the reader along and produce a small Aha moment, when things are clarified. These writers steer adroitly between the two reefs, producing a pleasurable read.

If you have the ability to do this already, then you certainly don't need this book. However, I believe you can take the strategies detailed herein, and with the help of good feedback, raise your work to that wonderful level of sophistication.

—Robert Qualkinbush,
Cross Junction, Virginia

THE IMPORTANCE OF THE OPENING

The slush pile reader is your gatekeeper to publication.

Daily she sits before a pile of manuscripts, let's say, a two-foot-tall stack. If she doesn't get through it, the pile will grow. Otherwise, she'll take the work home on nights and weekends. Given these conditions, it is only realistic that you, as a writer, have just 13 to 38 lines to persuade her you are a professional. 13 lines is what she'll read on the first page, then you have maybe 24 more if she turns the page.

If.

In order to make the "first cut," you must persuade her that you have the craft to be paid for it.

As storytellers we tend to think in terms of scenes, and this is a good thing. Memorable scenes appear to be the basic building blocks of good fiction. But when it comes to speculative fiction we find an interesting phenomenon: most beginners jump straight into a scene. Just scan through the openings in any given week on the Critters Workshop site or scan the Fragments and Feedback for Short Works forum on the Hatrack River website. I'd say 90% or more of these stories begin with a scene.

So what's the problem with this?

The problem is that 85% openings by professionals begin with "situational" information. They open with "telling" to set up the first scene. Whether these spec fiction pros did this out of instinct, good editing, or pure luck is irrelevant. The fact stands that almost all professionally published short fiction, in the science fiction or fantasy genres, DO NOT jump straight into a scene. (For those who wish a more precise definition, a "scene" has cascades of stimulus and response which occur in real-time.)

With more than 90% of amateurs' spec stories, the first words plunge you straight into a scene. By contrast, only 15% of published spec fiction in the "Big Three" magazines, that is, F&SF, Asimov's, and Analog, begin this way. These stories use "telling," or an epigram, or a poem, or some other method to help set up the first scene.

As want-to-be professionals, this fact should give us pause.

An established author has a relationship to both the audience and the editor. As readers, we're willing to work a little if the opening is a bit slow or confusing. It's kind of like listening to a beloved relative drone on a bit before they get to the point. You'll be polite, you'll give them the benefit of the doubt. The same thing applies to the work of an established author, because a familiar relationship exists.

As a beginning author, you won't be given the benefit of the doubt. It behooves you therefore, to know how pro short fiction actually begins. If you'd asked me, before I began this study, whether most pro short fiction opened with a scene. I'd have said, "Of Course!" But in fact, the very first words most of us read are "set-up" for the crucial first scene. We're all subject to a natural form of selective memory. We tend to remember fiction in terms of bits of scenes. The scene is what we remember, not the "telling" that set it up.

Just as an example, I grabbed, at random, a copy of **Realms of Fantasy, Analog and Asimov's** from my bookshelf. Here are the first two sentences from each story therein. My comments are in brackets.

Realms of Fantasy, April 2007

> Any sensible person would have many critical things to say of Kenji the priest: He drank too much.
>
> – *A Touch of Hell*, Richard Parks, p. 36.

[Note: no scene]

The rope was braided out of common halfa-grass, as many ropes are in the Antique Lands. It trailed from a low and broad basket, made of doum-palm fibers but unworthy of any further remark.

– *The Rope: a New Tale of the Antique Lands,* Noreen Doyle, p.46.

[Note: while quite visual, we find out in the next sentences that this rope has been laying about for five days, hence this cannot be considered a scene, but visual "telling."]

Stanton, Texas - October 1989

It's easy to get girls when you play the guitar.

At least in a nothing town like mine.

– *Stephanie Shrugs,* Josh Rountree, p.52.

[no scene]

A voice inside Becca's head told her not to look but she did anyway. The mare had snorted violently followed by Bill's garbled exclamation.

– *Black Jack Davy,* Trent Hergenrader, p.56.

[the scene begins after the first sentence]

There it is again.

I lick my lips and try to see who could be crying out there in the woods.

– *Red,* Jackie Kessler, p.64.

[the scene begins after the first sentence]

Some she found in old digs, and there's always a line of them in antique shop windows: one for a dollar. I used to buy one for her every week, coming home from grocery shopping, but that was before Marc left.

– *Bottles*, Samantha Henderson, p. 68.

[no scene]

> 1. Dreams have power. Not the common dreams of flying or arriving naked at work— those are nothing more than the froth thrown up as sleep waves roll across the mind.
>
> – *The Tao of Crocodiles,* Euan Harvey, p.80.

[no scene]

Analog, November 1998

> Excerpt from the TELES Journal of Eponan Field Ecology, Currents Column, Vol. 14, No. 3, January 16, 2265 (Earth):
>
> A suspected dracowolf was sighted by a hydrology team last week.
>
> – *Duel for a Dracowolf,* Wolf Reed, p.10.

[no scene]

> The trouble with planets is, they're big. I never really thought about it much when I was living on one—nor after I'd died, for that matter—but they're huge.
>
> It's not intuitively obvious.

– *Kissing Cousins*, Jerry Oltion, p.43.

[no scene]

It is such a little thing. A squiggly little line that invariably causes many a Spockian raised eyebrow when relaying a web address to resistant web-o-phobes.

– *Waltzing my Tilde*, F. Alexander Brejcha, p.54

[no scene]

PROLOGUE

Behold sayeth the King
Is all lost already?
Blown away on the winds,
a desert
to remain
until all memory
of the race
is
gone!

The last rays of the dying sun cast long shadows into the crevices where Bob was working.

–*Wrench and Claw*, S.D. Howe, p. 58

[Note: we only get scenic data after the opening poem]

Cue drones: carrier harmonics at 131, 220, and 440 Hz.

They stand, heads bowed beneath black umbrellas, rain rolling off in steady streams to pool around their shoes.

–*The Dream of Nations,* Wil McCarthy, p.96

[Note: once again the scenic information occurs after the material in italics]

Arachne was a spiderweb spinning in space. Her strands were fullerene wire, cylindrical molecules of pure carbon a trillion trillion atoms long.

–*Aggravated Vehicular Genocide*, Christopher L. Bennet, p. 110.

[Note: visual info followed by exposition; note also that the author did not have to specify that *Arachne* is a spacecraft—the information is implied; this category of implied information will helps us to sift what info we'll need in an opening]

Asimov's Science Fiction, Sept. 1999

> Joseph is a smart man, and a sullen man, and skeptical. All qualities that Emma appreciates, and accepts, and finds intriguing, in that order.
>
> – *Nodaway*, Robert Reed, p.16.

[Pure situational information focusing on character and relationship]

> Tan says they intend to give us all some kind of painful disease. He claims he overheard them talking about it when they brought him here.
>
> – *The Scientific Community,* Lois Tilton, p.40.

[Not scenic, pure situational info]

> For the first four years of his life, Alec Checkerfield wore a life vest.
>
> This was so that if he accidentally went over the side of his parents' yacht, he would be guaranteed a rescue.
>
> – *Smart Alec*, Kage Baker, p. 50.

[while a life vest is concrete and visual, this does not make this scenic, since it's not taking place in real-time]

> As soon as the sound of Sloth's wake up call speared it's way into my ever-so-pleasant dream, before I was even awake, I knew that the Dead Cat Squad had come to call again—and I was instantly afraid, not for myself, but for Cade.
>
> Carol-Anne woke up too, and forced her eyes open while I was hauling myself from the sheets and groping for a deadgown to hide my sexsuit.
>
> – *Hidden Agendas*, Brian Stableford, p.70.

[A scenic opening that follows the criteria in a later section "opening with a scene"]

> Human beings call me Mustardseed. As satellites of Uranus go, I wasn't much—barely three kilometers in radius compared to Titania's five hundred or so.
>
> –*Mustardseed*, G. David Nordley, p. 100.

[Not scenic]

> There was a girl named Helwar Ahl. Her family lived on an island north and east of the Second Continent, which was known in those days as the Great Southern Continent.
>
> –*Dapple: A Hwarath Romance,* Eleanor Arnason, p. 104.

[Not scenic]

I've left out **F&SF**, simply because I think these examples illustrate my point. Of these nineteen openings, only two use a "scenic" first sentence. Those are:

> As soon as the sound of Sloth's wake up call speared it's way into my ever-so-pleasant dream, before I was even awake, I knew that the Dead Cat Squad had come

> to call again—and I was instantly afraid, not for myself, but for Cade.
>
> – *Hidden Agendas*, Brian Stableford, p.70.

And

> *Arachne* was a spiderweb spinning in space.
>
> – *Aggravated Vehicular Genocide*, Christopher L. Bennet, p. 110.

The rest of these stories begin by giving other kinds of information – situational or character-related information.

In order to conceptualize the difference between an opening in a non-spec fiction story versus a spec fiction story, we'll use the metaphor of a funnel shown in Fig. 1. The width of the funnel mouth indicates the fundamental difference between spec fiction and other types of fiction. In spec fiction the ordinary "rules" of the universe may be radically different. It's one of the reasons we as spec fiction readers like imaginative fiction. In a "mundane" story, we only have a trickle of information that the reader needs to know before we proceed into the first scene. By contrast, spec fiction is like pouring a huge jug of water into a small tube. Anyone who's changed the oil on their car knows what can happen (especially if it's one of those big 4-quart jugs and you're pouring into an oil hole about the same size and the stuff gushes and blorps all around the hole and over the engine—Okay, so I *don't* use a funnel when I do this, I admit it!)

Fig. 1, THE OPENING "DATA FUNNEL"
The challenge of opening a *non*-spec fiction story versus a spec fiction story

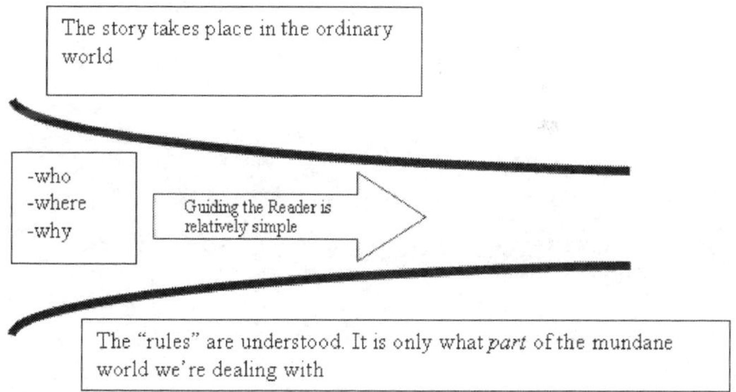
Fig 1.a The *Non-spec* fiction story
The story takes place in the ordinary world
-who
-where
-why
Guiding the Reader is relatively simple
The "rules" are understood. It is only what *part* of the mundane world we're dealing with

Fig 1.b The Spec fiction story

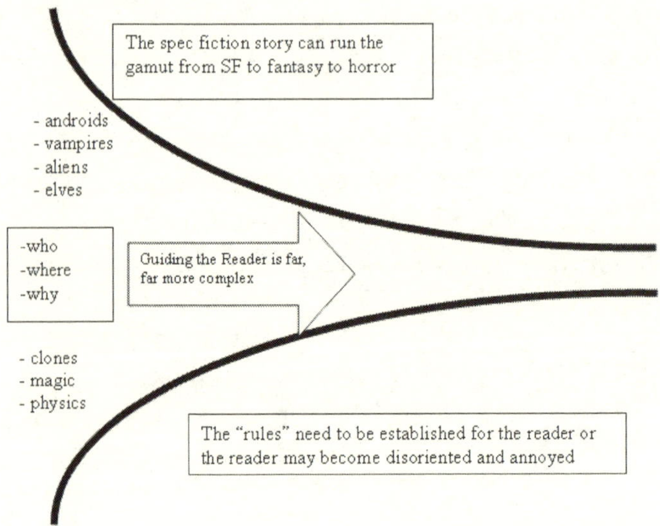
The spec fiction story can run the gamut from SF to fantasy to horror
- androids
- vampires
- aliens
- elves
-who
-where
-why
Guiding the Reader is far, far more complex
- clones
- magic
- physics
The "rules" need to be established for the reader or the reader may become disoriented and annoyed

In this metaphor, "spillage," spilling oil over the engine, is losing the reader through confusion.

So what is the problem with starting with a scenic opening when you have a lot of situational information that the reader needs to know?

Here's an example of the biggest problem. I've created this story as an example. My reactions as a reader are in *italics*:

> She swam among the coral. Above her, Tom's boat cast a shadow against the bottom.

> *[Okay, so this woman is probably a scuba diver. Tom is her husband or boyfriend.]*
>
> Splashing sounds from overhead signaled Tom's entrance into the water. He slowly descended toward her, air from his scuba gurgling, sending up in silvery bursts. She could see him smiling around his mouthpiece as he drew near. He removed the mouthpiece and placed a kiss on her lips.
>
> *[Huh? How can he kiss her if she doesn't remove the mouthpiece from her own mouth? Or did the writer just skip this?]*
>
> He playfully tugged at her tail fin.
>
> *[What?? Okay, is she a mermaid? An intelligent fish??]*

In this hypothetical example, the author has violated one of Orson Scott Card's "Three Don'ts" - Don't Confuse. As a reader, I expect that the writer to have enough professional skill to not confuse me in the very opening of her story. The POV character is a mermaid, yet this wasn't made clear from the very beginning. Some readers may have been "on track" with the writer's intentions, but a percentage, probably a large percentage, were not. Figure 2 illustrates what's going on in this story.

Fig. 2
"Spillage" in the funnel metaphor

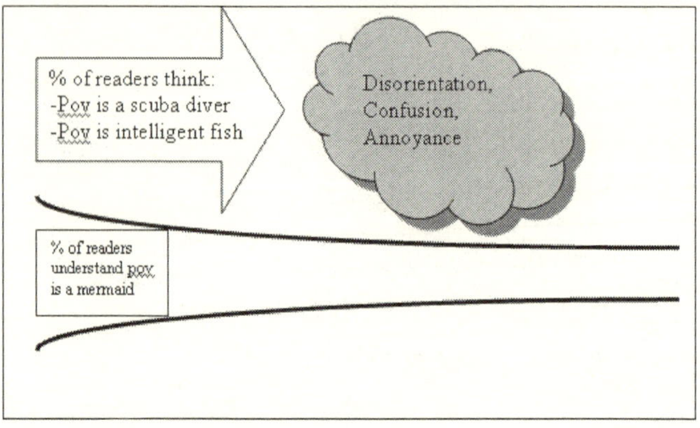

A clearer version of the above text might be:

> Two fathoms below the surface, waiting for her lover to arrive, she began to get petulant. She'd combed her hair with a sea urchin brush and now the tresses floated nicely. She'd polished her scales for the third time with a sea sponge, wringing the last of the slimy polish from the dying creature. Tom's boat floated overhead, casting a shadow on the sandy

> bottom. He would be putting on the cumbersome body-machinery that let him breathe in her world.

The challenge of the spec fiction opening is far greater than that faced by a writer of "mundane" fiction; the spec opening requires the combining of visual information and a *huge burden of situational information* into a smooth flow. Beginners tend to leave out vital situational information. Here are just a few actual examples of situational info that I've seen dropped from beginners' stories:

- The focal character is an angel
- The focal character is psychic
- The focal character is a demon
- The world is artificial
- The world combines technology and "fantasy" elements

Often, the reader is going along with a story and winds up feeling bushwacked by such information. The result is annoyance. An additional result is: no sale.

SPECULATIVE FICTION PROTOCOLS

As writers of spec fiction, we have one advantage: there are "reading protocols" that work to our advantage. In the re-written passage about the mermaid above, I have given facts that imply what the POV character is, and the reader can make inferences that she's a mermaid. The following passage illustrates a principle used in SF and fantasy that can be helpful:

> We marched nineteen miles today. This is our third long hike from the coast, where the ghoaps gathered us at their Villa Ventoriel.
>
> We are fewer than two hundred survivors, all catamaran sailors. The merlows cut the anchor lines of our Leader's fleet in advance of the storm, and our frigates foundered far from sight of land because of their draught. But the catamarans were designed as landing craft. The seas drove us, white with submerged perils, and some vessels reached shore despite our unsprung rudders. And despite merlow attacks. There are many reefs in the Lowland Sea, like teeth inside teeth. We bent to our skills and exhausted ourselves, but

> it was the luck of the wind which ones made it.
>
> Those who offered resistance to the ghoap beach patrols—they too were slaughtered. We are the few who came ashore too weak and isolated. A fraction. A small shamed fraction of a dead majority.
>
> —*The Valley of the Humans,* Phillip C. Jennings, **Asimov's**, Nov. '94, p.238.

Now what exactly is a "ghoap"? What's a "merlow"? Experienced SF and fantasy readers will hold these terms in abeyance, trusting that the author will fill us in more fully in due time. Orson Scott Card writes,

> This principle of abeyance is one of the protocols of reading speculative fiction that makes it difficult for some people who aren't familiar with the genre to grasp what's going on...
>
> ...the reader who is inexperienced in sf thinks that the author expects him to already know what the term means. He stops cold, trying to guess what the term means from its context. But he can't guess,

because there isn't enough context yet. Instead of holding the information in abeyance like a small mystery, he is just as likely to think that either the writer is so clumsy that she doesn't know how to communicate well, or that this novel is so esoteric that its readers are expected to know uncommon terms that aren't even in the dictionary.

This is one of the real boundaries between sf and non-sf writing. Science fiction and fantasy writers handle exposition this way, by dropping in occasional terms...and explaining them only later. The sf reader doesn't expect to receive a complete picture of the world all at once. Rather he builds up his own picture bit by bit from clues within the text.

–*How to Write Science Fiction and Fantasy,*" Orson Scott Card, 1990, Writer's Digest Books, p. 91.

Many beginners, myself included, like to begin stories, not only with scenes, but with action scenes. The following is a butchered version of the opening of the short story *The War Memorial* by Allen Steele published in the Sept. '95 issue of **Asimov's**. I've hacked away all summarized information and left just the stimulus-response cascades. Note how confusing this piece is without "telling."

> Giordano hears the pilot scream one last obscenity before his ugly spacecraft is reduced to metal rain, then something slams against his back and everything goes black. When the lights flicker back on within his soft cocoon and the flatscreen directly in front of his face stops fuzzing, he sees that a few dozen meters away at three o'clock, there's a new crater that used to be Robinson.
>
> Sgt. Boyle's voice comes through the comlink, shouting orders. Traveling overwatch, due west, head for Marker One-Eight-Five. Kemp, take Robinson's position. Cortez, you're point. Stop staring, Giordano (yes sir). Move, move, move.
>
> Giordano is sweating hard, his breath coming in ragged gasps…
>
> –from *The War Memorial*, Allen Steele, Asimov's, Sept. 1995, p. 74.

Most people have to re-read the first few sentences to get an idea of what is going on. What follows is the original. Note in the original how much summary, that is, "telling," is taking place, even in an action sequence.

> The first-wave assault is jinxed from the very beginning. Even before the dropship touches down, its pilot shouts over the comlink that a Pax missile battery seven klicks away has locked in on their position, despite the ECM buffer set up by the lunarsats. So it's going to be a dustoff; the pilot has done his job by getting the men down to the surface, and he doesn't want to be splattered across Mare Tranquillitatis.
>
> It doesn't matter anyway. Baker Company has been deployed for less than two minutes before the Pax heatseekers pummel the ground around them and take out the dropship even as it begins its ascent.
>
> Giordano hears the pilot scream one last obscenity before his ugly spacecraft is reduced to metal rain, then something slams against his back and everything within the suit goes black. For an instant he believes he's dead, that he's been nailed by one of the heatseekers, but it's just debris from the dropship. The half-ton ceramic-polymer shell of the Mark III Valkyrie Combat Armor Suit has absorbed the brunt of the impact.

When the lights flicker back on within his soft cocoon and the flat- screen directly in front of his face stops fuzzing, he sees that not everyone has been so lucky. A few dozen meters away at three o'clock, there's a new crater that used to be Robinson. The only thing left of Baker Company's resident card cheat is the severed rifle arm of his CAS.

He doesn't have time to contemplate Robinson's fate. He's in the midst of battle. Sgt. Boyle's voice comes through the comlink, shouting orders. Traveling overwatch, due west, head for Marker One-Eight-Five. Kemp, take Robinson's position. Cortez, you're point. Stop staring, Giordano (yes sir). Move, move, move.

So they move, seven soldiers in semi-robotic heavy armor, bounding across the flat silver-gray landscape. Tin men trying to outrun the missiles plummeting down around them, the soundless explosions the missiles make when they hit. For several kilometers around them, everywhere they look, there are scores of other tin men doing the same, each trying to survive a silent hell called the Sea of Tranquillity.

> Giordano is sweating hard, his breath coming in ragged gasps...
>
> – *The War Memorial,* Allen Steele, Asimov's, Sept. 1995, p. 74.

Note that summary can, and often does, contain visual information. It is often hard for an unpracticed eye, to spot that this is "telling." Here's the original of *The War Memorial* with the "telling" elements in italics `Courier New font` for clarity:

> `The first-wave assault is jinxed from the very beginning. Even before the dropship touches down, its pilot shouts over the comlink that a Pax missile battery seven klicks away has locked in on their position, despite the ECM buffer set up by the lunarsats. So it's going to be a dustoff; the pilot has done his job by getting the men down to the surface, and he doesn't want to be splattered across Mare Tranquillitatis.`
>
> It doesn't matter anyway. Baker Company has been deployed for less than two

minutes before the Pax heatseekers pummel the ground around them and take out the dropship even as it begins its ascent.

Giordano hears the pilot scream one last obscenity before his ugly spacecraft is reduced to metal rain, then something slams against his back and everything within the suit goes black. *For an instant he believes he's dead, that he's been nailed by one of the heatseekers, but it's just debris from the dropship. The half-ton ceramic-polymer shell of the Mark III Valkyrie Combat Armor Suit has absorbed the brunt of the impact.*

When the lights flicker back on within his soft cocoon and the flat- screen directly in front of his face stops fuzzing, he sees *that not everyone has been so lucky*. A few dozen meters away at three o'clock, there's a new crater that used to be Robinson. The only thing left of *Baker Company's resident card cheat* is the severed rifle arm of his CAS.

He doesn't have time to contemplate Robinson's fate. He's in the midst of battle. Sgt. Boyle's voice comes through the comlink, shouting orders. Traveling overwatch, due west, head for Marker One-Eight-

Five. Kemp, take Robinson's position. Cortez, you're point. Stop staring, Giordano (yes sir). Move, move, move.

So they move, seven soldiers in semi-robotic heavy armor, bounding across the flat silver-gray landscape. Tin men trying to outrun the missiles plummeting down around them, the soundless explosions the missiles make when they hit. For several kilometers around them, everywhere they look, there are scores of other tin men doing the same, each trying to survive a silent hell called the Sea of Tranquillity.

Giordano is sweating hard, his breath coming in ragged gasps…

– *The War Memorial,* Allen Steele, Asimov's, Sept. 1995, p. 74.

OPENING STRATEGIES

SIFTING YOUR STORY INFORMATION

The purpose of the following is to help you winnow down options in your opening to one or two possibilities that might work. It's not, as with anything creative, fool-proof. To begin:

- What is the "heart" of the story?
- What situational information does the reader need to know up front?
- What information can be deferred or implied?
- What information can be skipped?

What is the "Heart" of the story?

How does one determine what information to put in a situational opening? In the first place, you must determine: what is the "heart" of your story? Figure 3 illustrates the relationship between the spec idea and the other elements of the story. In most cases there will be a primary relationship, say, between the spec idea and the characters, or the spec idea and the setting. A useful tool is also thinking about your ending.

What is the ending? What about your ending, if altered, would utterly destroy your story? The ending is what determines the 'heart' of a story. Thus the emotional feel of the story should be reflected in the opening. A horror story shouldn't mislead the reader with light farce in the opening.

Figure 3. The relationship of Spec Idea to other story elements

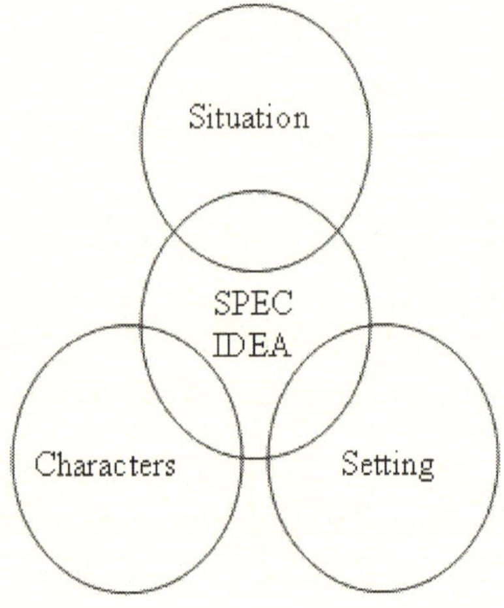

Yet this idealized relationship can lead to huge complexity. Figure 4 illustrates the overlap between the spec idea and the other elements of the story. The writer of non-spec fiction faces no such challenge. It's no surprise that spec fiction

beginners should find the opening especially challenging.

Figure 4. complexity of overlap between Spec Idea and Story Elements

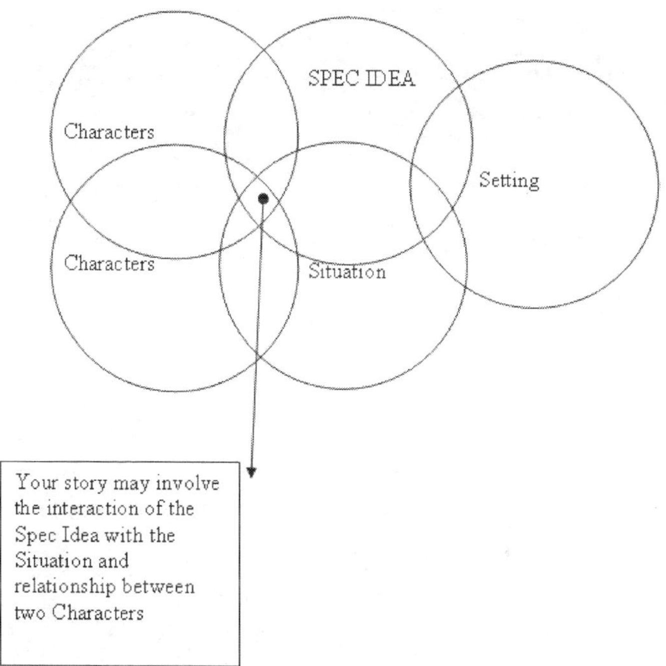
SPEC IDEA
Characters
Setting
Characters
Situation
Your story may involve the interaction of the Spec Idea with the Situation and relationship between two Characters

Here are two examples of scenic openings in which the spec idea can be illustrated in the first sentence:

> It was hot on the beach, so Suetork spread herself nearly flat, her transparent sphere becoming a ring of what appeared to be damp sand. She scattered her black eyes around like pebbles, on the watch for predators who might
>
> – *The Shape of Things to Come*, Marianne Dyson, Analog, Mar 1996, p. 76.

(Note: The "heart" of Marianne Dyson's story is about an alien first contact, in which the alien mimics the shape and sound of a human child.)

And:

> The Spook was peeling off from orbit, headed for Washington, DC, and it felt just great.
>
> – *Spook*, Bruce Sterling, **F&SF**, April 1983 p. 53.

Like many cyberpunk stories, *Spook* is about a dehumanized main character. The fact that peeling off from orbit "felt just great" is the first hint that something is "off" about this character. A sentence or two later, Sterling describes the glow of re-entry as a "cheery red." The Spook of the title is an industrial spy. Another author, given the idea of future industrial espionage, might place the actions of espionage at the "heart" of such a story. In this case, Sterling's emphasis is on the character, a fey sociopath who lives his life mediated by a bio/cyber brain interface known as the Veil. His reactions, personality and memories — his very "self" is barely human.

It is helpful to then analyze the following aspects of your story:

a) Spec idea
b) Situation info
c) Setting info
d) Character/relationship info

Of each of these categories you must ask yourself: should the information be dramatized? Can it be deferred until later? Does it need to be upfront and told before the scene, lest confusion result? Is it the "heart" of the story? We as readers tend to have a "default setting" when it comes to story elements. For example, an outdoor setting will take place in clement weather unless we're told otherwise. Similarly, we assume characters are "normal," that is, average humans, unless told otherwise.

If the "heart" of the story is relational, then Character/relationship info should probably take the lead. If the spec idea cannot be deferred (as in the case of the "mermaid" example given above) then one should probably lead with that.

Let's look at some examples. Table 1 lists spec idea relationships in the three spec ideas in Sean McMullen's novelette, *Enigma*. Both the spec idea and the setting are one in the same. Character and Relationship information are not at the heart of the story. There are three spec ideas in "Enigma." The first is the planet Enigma itself. The second spec idea is that the astronauts have animal genes grafted into their genomes to enhance certain survival traits. The third idea is "echo" technology. In McMullen's universe, space travel is a "one way trip." Echo technology beams memories back to a duplicate clone body on Earth. When the body on the space trip dies, the clone is unfrozen and the person continues their life on Earth. Here are the spec ideas tabulated:

Table 1, spec ideas in Sean McMullen's Enigma, breakdown and presentation analysis

Spec ideas, Enigma	**Does it need up-front explication to avoid reader confusion?**	**Telling: ease? + Storytelling problems & preferences**	**Showing: ease? + Storytelling problems & preferences**	**Implicit in genre**
(Character) Humans with animal genes	no; defer this till later	easy; straight exposition would be fine, but probably better dramatized	easy; can be done in character interactions	No
(Situational) Echo technology	no; defer this till later	easy; no	easy; dramatizing would be outside the scope of this story	No
(Setting) **The planet Enigma = HEART OF STORY**; up-front info required to avoid confusion; however, a scenic treatment of scientists writing a report on Enigma would be lame, boring and use a lot of words; so we are left with the summarizing power of "telling."				Yes (it's an alien planet, a standard trope of SF)

Figures 4 a,b, and c are Venn diagrams of McMullen's two main spec ideas:

Fig. 4a. Relationship of Spec Idea-to-Setting in Sean McMullen's Enigma

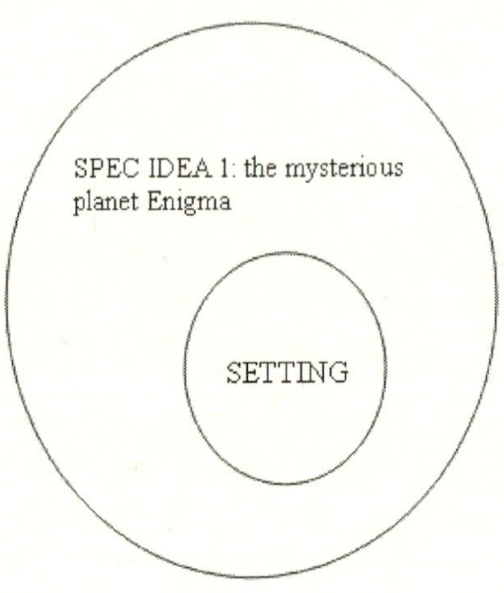

Fig. 4b. Spec Idea of Humans gene-spliced with animal survival traits in Sean McMullen's Enigma

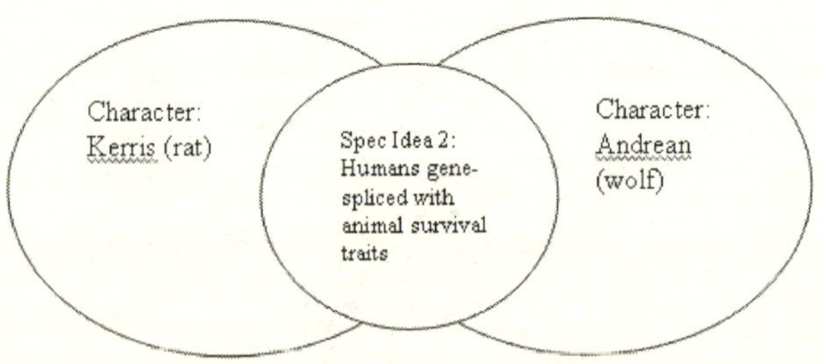

Figure 4c. Both main spec ideas of Sean McMullen's Enigma combined

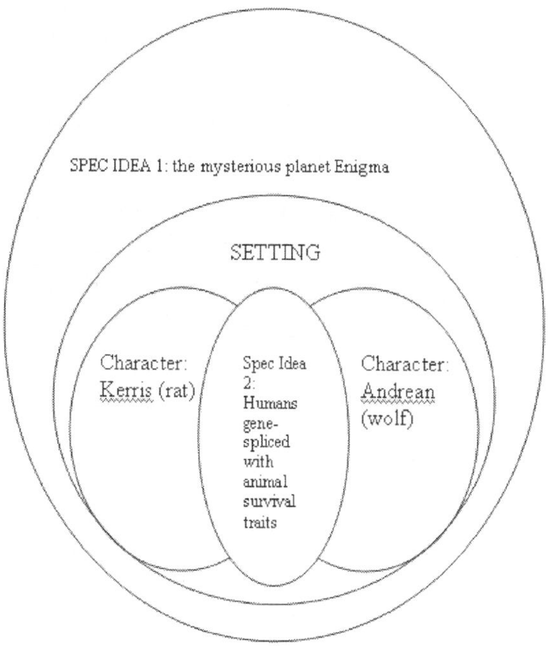

Enigma requires both up-front explication and is also at the heart of the story. Telling is the more efficient method. One can't have three scenes of scientists discussing probe images and writing a report. Boring. Thus McMullen begins his story with:

> Enigma hung beneath us like a mighty display screen in space, alive with colors, yet showing no picture that we could un-

> derstand. There were no seas, mountains, or polar caps; neither were there clouds or forests. There was, however, a city. The entire planetary surface was a vast, empty, incomprehensible city. It was a city that could not be lived in, our robotic probes had told us that. All its surfaces were curves, arches, light wells, and tunnels. There were no roads or walkways, the mighty halls had no floors that could be walked on, the towers were hollow, and there were no rooms, offices, balconies, windows, or steps. Because the material of the city absorbed radio-frequency signals, our probes had been lost when they went deeper than one mile into the caverns and tunnels.
>
> – *Enigma,* Sean McMullen, Analog, January-February, 2011 (electronic version) p.179.

Once we have this information up-front, McMullen can then use character interaction combined with exposition to scenically deal with his second spec idea: humans gene-spliced with animal traits.

> Andrean was slightly wolf, and was commander of the lander Cumulus. Five

of us would share a space no bigger than a small apartment until we died, but that was no problem. We would not live long.

I was a woman who was somewhat rat. The other three had traces of terrier in their DNA. An alpha wolf, an ultraloyal pack, and an outsider—me. Someone's computer model had once concluded that it was the near-perfect exploration team.

"Too soon, our turn," Andrean said as we waited for the launch window.

There was a certain quality of gloom in his voice. It told me that he did not like taking chances, and that was reassuring.

"You don't sound happy," I prompted.

"Clever Kerris Rat. This star's planetary system has no precedent. That worries me."

"Why? Nine other systems have two gas giants and a single rocky planet."

We had been engineered to disagree without actually coming to blows because that was the current theory of team dynamics. We were also just a little repelled by each other sexually, which simplified interpersonal relations.

"For anyone frightened of meteor impact, Enigma is really configured to last," Andrean replied.

> "Configured? Who could configure an entire system?"
>
> "Who indeed, but the evidence suggests it. Here the gas giants have no moons or rings, and there are no asteroids, comets, or even meteors. Dust is at the levels of interstellar space. Enigma's orbit even leaves it untouched when the star eventually swells into a red giant."
>
> I knew all of that, but it did not worry me. Wolf paranoia is different from rat paranoia because rats live their lives in danger. Rats have dwelt in the shadows of a more advanced species ever since humans evolved, but wolves live separately, in wilderness.
>
> – *Enigma,* Sean McMullen, Analog, January-February 2011, p.179.

In Richard Parks' fantasy-mystery, "A Touch of Hell," the story takes place in medieval Japan. The spec idea draws from Japanese folklore. It's the idea of animal-to-human transformation or the reverse; human beings can transform into animals or monsters due to strong emotion. The mystery story requires, according to Dorothy L. Sayers, a certain emotional detachment by the detective. So the "heart" of a mystery is rarely about the crime, but rather about characters surrounding the crime. At the heart of *A Touch of Hell* is the growing camaraderie between Lord Yamada and the priest, Kenji.

Table 2. Spec ideas in A Touch of Hell, by Richard Parks, breakdown and presentation analysis

Spec ideas, A Touch of Hell	**Does it need up-front explication to avoid reader confusion?**	**Telling: ease? + Storytelling problems & preferences**	**Showing: ease? + Storytelling problems & preferences**	**Implicit in genre**
Animal-to-human transformation	no; defer this till later	easy; but lame as straight exposition: "transformations between animals and humans happened all the time in medieval Japan."	Easy; could be done in small scene	No, this idea is quite alien to western culture
Human-to-animal transformation due to strong emotion	no; defer this till later	Same situation, easy; but lame as straight exposition	easy; could be done in a scene or in character interactions	No, this idea is quite alien to western culture
(Characters/relationships) Camaraderie between Lord Yamada and Kenji = **HEART OF STORY**; We can start with the heart of the story scenically				

As with any hard-drinking detective, someone needs to bring Lord Yamada the case.

> Any sensible person would have many critical things to say of Kenji the priest: He drank too much. He didn't bathe often, ritually or otherwise. His understanding

of and devotion to the Eightfold Way was dubious at best. Yet let it never be said he couldn't recognize the obvious.

"Yamada-san, you look terrible."

Kenji kneeled, grinning, in the doorway to my rooms, neither quite in nor quite out, much like his relative position on spiritual matters. The open door let in a shaft of light, illuminating an empty sake cask, the remnants of my last drinking cup—smashed when I finally realized that the cask was empty—and me, lying on top of some not very clean bedding. I groaned and tried to sit up, but the room was still spinning too much. I settled for groaning again.

"Who let you in?"

"And a cheery good morning to you as well. The Widow Tamahara saw no need to announce me, since we're old friends."

"I've known you a long time. It's not the same thing."

Kenji had a more proper Buddhist name he'd been given when he'd become a priest, but he didn't use it. His priest-name was something pure and pious, no doubt, which were attributes I could never quite associate with Kenji.

He grinned. "Even so," he said, and then the grin went away and he went on,

> "It doesn't help, you know. The sake, I mean."
>
> I tried to sit up, but had to move slowly. My head felt like a blowfish looks. "What do you want? I know you didn't come here to lecture me on the evils of drinking, you of all people."
>
> "You need employment, if nothing else to pay for these elegant quarters and more useless drink. I may have something for you."
>
> – *A Touch of Hell*, Richard Parks, Realms of Fantasy, April, 2007, p. 36.

Since the spec ideas can be deferred, Parks has it illustrated in the second scene. As Lord Yamada and Kenji journey to an isolated monastery beset by an ogre, Parks dramatizes one of the spec ideas, and has the characters discussing the second spec idea:

> I followed Kenji off the road at a place that might have been a path but really looked more like a slight gap in the trees. Yet the way was clear and before long I heard the sounds of a waterfall. I also heard something else. A glance at Kenji

showed that he had heard the same thing—the unmistakable music of female laughter.

"It seems this place is not quite so unknown as you thought."

Kenji just grinned and plunged ahead at a trot. I sighed and followed at a more leisurely pace. I arrived at the pool to be greeted with the following tableau: Kenji standing just at the edge of the water and beyond him two naked young women clinging to each other in the deepest part of the pool just beyond where the mountain stream feeding the pool splashed down from the hillside.

From their clothes draped neatly over a pair of bushes on the opposite shore, it was obvious that they were two young and perhaps foolish peasant girls from some nearby village or farm. Still, their rustic origins seemed to have done them no harm: their hair was long and black, their skin the color of golden straw in autumn. Their lithe bodies were demurely veiled by the water, but only just, and they indeed made a lovely sight.

They looked at us with the appropriate mixture of surprise and apprehension, but their dark eyes did not agree with what their faces were telling us.

"Ladies, have no fear—" Kenji began, but I interrupted him.

"Ladies," I said, "you're wasting your time. This alleged monk has no piety to tempt, and as for me, I barely have any soul left at all worth mentioning."

One of the women actually snarled at me. In another instant they disappeared under the water, nimble as a pair of minnows. There was a ripple and splash on the opposite shore as two red fox vixens emerged from the pool, shook off the water, and vanished into the trees. Their clothes, of course, had disappeared; they were never really there.

Kenji stared at me. "They ... foxes? How did you know?"

I shrugged. "Let's just say I've gotten better at spotting them over the years. So. Will you unpack the rice cakes or shall I?"

Kenji went searching through his pack, muttering all the while. I skirted the edge of the pool to the waterfall, caught some of the splashing water in my hands, and drank. It was clean and cold and, unlike the women, very real. Still, I found myself wishing there was enough magic clinging to the place to transform the water to wine. I put the thought away.

By the time I returned, Kenji had the rice cakes arranged on a small cloth and had already eaten one. I took a couple for myself. While I ate I noticed Kenji staring wistfully at the water.

"I suppose I should thank you," he said. "Yet, honestly, what's the worst that could have happened?"

"They might have kept you entranced with their lovely selves for an afternoon from your perspective, only to discover that, back on the road, several hundred years had passed. Or.

"Or?"

"Or they might have been bathing together in human form for a lark, and been so very angry at being disturbed that they would have killed and eaten you and left your bones to molder at the bottom of this pool."

"Oh." Kenji seemed to consider this. "I'm not so keen on that option. Still, maybe it would have been worth the risk to find out."

"Not for me," I said. "I don't trust anything that can change at a whim."

"Then you don't trust human beings in general," Kenji said.

I had no argument with that. "Certainly not. Why would I trust any creature that can take a perfectly useful form of its own and let jealousy change it into, say, a snake?"

Kenji frowned. "I knew about foxes, of course, but a human transformation? I thought that was just a legend."

"Why? Doesn't your own tradition tell of a once-pious monk who was so overcome with lust for the daughter of an Emperor that he changed into a rat? Some emotions are too powerful for a human form to contain."

Kenji had just taken a big bite of one of the rice cakes and he chewed, looking thoughtful. "I assume you're referring to the story of the priest Raigo of Mii Temple," he said when his mouth was no longer quite so full. "That's just a story they tell to frighten the young monks."

"Suit yourself. Go seduce those foxes, for all I care. Just don't complain to me when one gets annoyed and bites your manhood off."

– *A Touch of Hell*, Richard Parks, Realms of Fantasy, April, 2007, p. 38-39.

David Brin's novel *Glory Season* posits a pastoral world in which males are a natural minority. To achieve this, feminist gengineers created a human subspecies in which the majority of the population are female clones. This cloning process is achieved without technological intervention. The minorities on this world are "normal" males and females with a father and mother's genes. The variant females are known as "vars." For Brin, it would seem that the heart of the story centers on the injustice suffered by minorities even in a pastoral world.

Table 3. Glory Season by David Brin, spec ideas, breakdown and presentation analysis

SPEC IDEAS	Up-front info needed to avoid confusion?	Telling: ease? + Storytelling problems & preferences	Showing: ease? + Storytelling problems & preferences
(situation) Majority of population are "hives" of female clones	No	Easy; however straight exposition would be lame, "In their world, hives of clones dominated society."	Easy; preferable to dramatize
(situation) Pastoral culture	Yes	Easy; can be implied	Easy; show in life-details
(setting) Terraformed alien world	Yes	Easy; can be implied or skipped; would be lame as an essay	Difficult; showing the terraforming would also make readers think story is about terraforming
"Natural" cloning	No	Medium difficulty; not very interesting as exposition	Large no. of words needed, but can be spread out over the first third of novel
That an engineered feminist utopia would still have injustice = HEART OF STORY, therefore it is the first scene. Telling can be used in the intro implying pastoral culture and alien world. Later in the scene dramatize that majority are "hives" of female clones			

Alien worlds are part-and-parcel of SF, so Brin merely implies it. *Glory Season* is a coming-of-age story in which the focal character, Maia, decides, in the end, to reject her culture. Thus Brin chooses to dramatize the "heart" of his novel, the injustice in relationships, even in a peaceful and pastoral culture. He must, however, establish that this takes place on an alien and probably terraformed world, and that the culture is pastoral:

> Twenty-six months before her second birthday, Maia learned the true difference between winter and summer.
>
> It wasn't simply the weather, or the way hot-season lightning storms used to crackle amid tall ships anchored in the harbor. Nor even the eye-tingling stab of Wengel— so distinct from other stars.
>
> The real difference was much more personal.
>
> "I can't play with you no more," her half sister, Sylvina, taunted one day. "'Cause you had a father!"
>
> "Did n-not!" Maia stammered, rocked by the slur, knowing that the word was vaguely nasty. Sylvie's rebuff stung, as if a bitter glacier wind blew through the crèche.
>
> "Did so! Had a father, dirty var!"
>
> "'Well . . . then you're a var, too!"
>
> The other girl laughed harshly. "Ha! I'm pure Lamai, just like my sisters, mothers an' grandmas. But you're a summer kid. That makes you U-neek. Var!"

Dismayed, too choked to speak, Maia could only watch Sylvina toss her tawny locks and flounce away, joining a cluster of children varied in age but interchangeable in appearance. Some unspoken ritual of separation had taken place, dividing the room. In the better half, over near the glowing hearth, each girl was a miniature, perfect rendition of a Lamai mother. The same pale hair and strong jaw. The same trademark stance with chin defiantly upraised.

Here on this side, the two boys were being tutored in their corner as usual, unaware of any changes that would scarcely affect them, anyway. That left eight little girls like Maia, scattered near the icy panes. Some were light or dark, taller or thinner. One had freckles, another, curly hair. What they had in common were their differences.

Maia wondered, Was this what it meant to have a *father*? Everyone knew summer kids were rarer than winterlings, a fact that once made her proud, till it dawned on her that being "special" wasn't so lucky, after all.

–*Glory Season*, David Brin, P. 1, 1993, Bantam.

Note that the situational idea that "Majority of population are 'hives' of female clones" *could* be dramatized fairly easily. Here is a re-write of Brin's opening. The symbols <|| indicate where there is a change or addition, ||> indicates the end of changes.

> Twenty-six months before her second birthday, Maia learned the true difference between winter and summer.
>
> It had nothing to do with the weather, or the way hot-season lightning storms crackled <|| in the harbor. Nor even the eye-tingling stab of Wengel— so distinct from other stars.
>
> It had everything to do with sexual reproduction, or rather, the lack of it.
>
> It happened while Maia kneeled before a toy harbor in the clan playroom. Sylvina, her half sister, snatched a wooden sextant from Maia's hands.
>
> "Hey! Give it back!"
>
> "I don't have to be nice to you," Sylvina taunted, then kicked over some of

> Maia's cargo ships, so the masts became entangled.
>
> "Stop it!"
>
> "I'm a Lamai," said Sylvie proudly.
>
> "So am I."
>
> "Nuh uh. You're only *half* Lamai—*you* had a *father*." ||>
>
> "Did n-not!" Maia stammered, rocked by the slur, knowing that the word was vaguely nasty. Sylvie's rebuff stung, as if a bitter glacier wind blew through the crèche.
>
> "Did so! Had a father, dirty var!"
>
> —*Glory Season*, David Brin, P. 1, 1993, Bantam.

I've removed "tall ships anchored in the harbor" and turned them into toy cargo ships with masts, and had Maia playing with a toy sextant—all to imply that this is a pastoral culture.

Now, this small change would make little difference. However, this dramatization of bullying might mislead the reader about the nature of the story. Some percentage of readers might get a "bad taste" in their mouths, anticipating that the entire novel will have victimization scenes.

However, the real risk in this example is that, as writers, we might want to make *everything* scenic. (I'll quote Orson Scott Card from his Literary Bootcamp lecture: "Whatever you want to be vivid, or remembered by the reader, Show; everything else, Tell.")

What information can be skipped?

What information can be skipped? In science fiction, space stations, space ships, aliens and alien worlds - these are so commonplace that one need not be that explicit, any more than you'd need to describe a saloon or a covered wagon to a reader of westerns.

CONTENT PATTERNS

Content patterns are methods of presenting information that recur in prose. Openings in spec fiction often follow a very discernable pattern, once one becomes aware of them. The following are a selection of content patterns one often sees in the openings of not just spec fiction, but many mainstream novels and short stories. Note that the content patterns can range in size:

- As small as a single word
- Clauses separated by commas
- Entire sentences or paragraphs

1) ORIENTATION/CHANGE

This pattern uses the following content: **<Orientation Tag> <Change Event>**

By orientation, I mean information the reader needs to orient themselves, often this takes the form of a time tag. Here is an example of a "clause separated" Content Pattern:

> Twenty-six months before her second birthday, Maia learned the true difference between winter and summer.

> – *Glory Season,* David Brin, P. 1, 1993, Bantam.

Broken down for clarity:

<Orientation Tag (time) >
Twenty-six months before her second birthday,
<Change Event> Maia learned the true difference between winter and summer.

Some more examples:

> For the first four years of his life, Alec Checkerfield wore a life vest.
>
> – *Smart Alec,* Kage Baker, **Asimov's,** Sept. 1999, p. 50.

> On Monday morning, a message waited on Sarah Lightburn's answering machine. It was Seule, breathless, forgetting to say when the call was made, or if she intended to call back.

– *The Fragrance of Orchids*, Sally McBride, **Asimov's**, May 1994, p.63.

On his eighteenth day in the tiger cage, Robert Stoney began to lose hope of emerging unscathed.

– *Oracle*, Greg Egan, **Asimov's** July 2000, p. 100.

On her sixth birthday, Moira laid her hand on the belly of a sick child, and the child was cured.

– *Three Gifts*, Dean Whitlock, **F&SF**, Feb. 1995, p. 67.

Ever since dad died, the sweet nothings stayed in Douglas's room.

– *Sweet Nothings*, Nina Kiriki Hoffman, **F&SF**, Aug 1998 , p. 137.

We reach him too late, pulling him out of the curing pond, nothing left but a melted body and a pain-twisted face.

> – *Due*, Robert Reed, **F&SF**, Feb., 2000, p.121.

The content pattern is sometimes reversed; that is:

<Change Event> <Orientation Tag>

> There comes a time in every rightly constructed girl's life when she has a raging desire to go somewhere and dig for buried treasure. This desire had come upon Jan Conway in the autumn of the year.
>
> – *Midnight Yearnings*, Rob Chilson, **F&SF** Aug. 1994, p. 33.

> They found him fifteen years later, exactly where his father had left him, in a box on a tall steel shelf in the warehouse.
>
> – *Dreamseed*, Carolyn Ives Gilman, **F&SF**, Oct/Nov., 2000, p.8.

The Orientation Tag can be spatial, as in:

> In Sarajevo, at Rade Koncar Square, Ahmo watched a young boy fall to the bullet of a sniper.
>
> – *Sarajevo,* Nick DiChario, **F&SF**, Mar. 1999, p. 95.

> When I came out of the pawnbroker's, I found that a little old man had chained his leg to the rim of one of my pushcart's wheels.
>
> – *For Every Tatter in its Mortal Dress*, Michael Shea, **F&SF**, Feb. 2000, p. 55.

Another very common content pattern in openings is the following:

ENVIRONMENT/ REACTION

2) <Environment affects character> <Character reaction>

> As soon as the sound of Sloth's wake up call speared it's way into my ever-so-pleasant dream, before I was even awake, I knew that the Dead Cat Squad had come

to call again—and I was instantly afraid, not for myself, but for Cade.

—*Hidden Agendas*, Brian Stableford, **Asimov's**, Sept. 1999, p.70.

The gale tore at him, and he felt its bite deep within, and he knew that if they did not make landfall in three days, that they would all be dead.

– *Shogun*, James Clavell, p. 1., Dell, 1986.

It was hot on the beach, so Suetork spread herself nearly flat, her transparent sphere becoming a ring of what appeared to be damp sand.

—*The Shape of Things to Come*, Marianne Dyson, **Analog**, Mar 1996, p. 76.

The Spook was peeling off from orbit, headed for Washington, DC, and it felt just great.

– *Spook*, Bruce Sterling, **F&SF**, April 1983 p. 53.

It began to grow cold in the cabin after the sun went down, and Nealy thought about building a fire.

– *The Promise of God,* Michael F. Flynn, **F&SF**, Mar. 1995, p.9.

It was the expression on the man's face that caught her gaze and made her stop to take a longer look at him.

– *The Cure for Love,* Brian Stableford, **Asimov's**, Mid-December, 1993, p. 10.

After her helicopter broke down in a dusty little a caravan town named Dzel, Lydia Duluth rented a *chool.*

– *Stellar Harvest,* Eleanor Arnasan, **Asimov's**, April 1999, p.104.

3) Again, the pattern can be reversed <Character Reaction> <Environment affects character>

> Chris Hudak knew he was in trouble when his computer bit him.
>
> – *Keyboard,* Harlan Ellison, **F&SF**, Jan., 1995, p. 43.

ONGOING ACTIVITY

A third Content Pattern is **<Ongoing Activity> <Change Event>.** Here are some short examples:

> A boy breaking deadwood in the forest saw God send two more future people to the time glade. He left his wood and crook and ran to tell the manor.
>
> – *Hypocaust and Bathysphere,* Rebecca Ore, **Asimov's** Jan. 1995, p. 126.

> All he can do at first is stare dully through the window at the barren Paleo-

zoic landscape. Then focus sharpens, his mind begins to work again, disbelief increases in inverse proportion to subsiding shock, and soon his thoughts seem to outrace the helicopter's shadow below. He constructs his first hypothesis: Somebody's made a terrible mistake.

– *The Wave Function Collapse*, Steven Utley, **Asimov's**, Mar., 2005, p. 52.

Crane was harrowing Hell when the call came.

– *Back Door Man*, Paul J. McAuley, **F&SF**, Mar., 1999, p.4.

The Town Council meeting was split down the middle—the Hullabaloo colonists on the one side and Fenella Elane Tyne on the other. Jerram stood in the back and admired the way Fenella strove to convince the tired farmers. Pacing around the podium, she brought to bear the power of unmatched intelligence, impeccable honesty, and polished verbal skills. In the discordant discussion that followed, Jerram studied her serious face. She was magnificent, but hopelessness coursed through him. She didn't have a chance of winning anyone over to her side. And he didn't stand a chance of winning her.

A red strobe light cut through the hall. Immediately the crowd silenced.

– *Hullabaloo,* Diane Turnshek, **Analog**, July/Aug., 2000, p.203.

Deep in the woods, gathering fungus for the Bone Witch's supper, Katya heard the firebird call her name.

– *Firebird,* R. Garcia y Robertson, **F&SF**, May, 2000, P. 126.

We were tooling along at four nine to c, when our captain came on the intercom to tell us we were being tailed.

– *An Ever-reddening Glow,* David Brin, **Analog**, Feb., 1996, p. 154.

As with the previous Content Patterns, it can be reversed:

> There were three of them— a tall one, and two shorter ones – and they appeared to Judith in the Day Room, where she was gazing through the barred windows, trying to figure out how to cable Diana, the 8-4 nurse, into returning her knitting needles so she could finish the sweater for Baby.
>
> – *Job's Partner,* Batya S. Yasgur & Barry N. Malzberg, **F&SF**, June, 1998, p. 83.

As I pointed out earlier, content patterns can be as short as a word or they can encompass entire sentences. As the story demands of visual information and backfill increase, one finds visuals and backfill interposing between the Ongoing Activity and the Change Event. Here are two examples of Ongoing Activity openings, both using the following pattern:

<Ongoing Activity> <Visuals> <Backfill> <<Begin Scene\ (Change Event)...

> Nothing moved except the searchers. In their shuttle they glided through the drowned forest, slipping over mats of wa-

terplants, around hummocks smothered in ferns, beneath the arching roots of songtrees. Vines looped from branch to branch, gnarled ropes of purple, like crude decorations that no one had bothered to take down. Far overhead the canopy of purple leaves formed a continuous lacework roof, admitting daylight in slivers of lavender.

The still waters divided at the prow of the shuttle, gathered again at the stern, and in a moment were still again. The eyes of the searchers ached. Their throats gagged on the steamy air. In only three days of hunting through the watery labyrinths of this vegetable planet they had grown weary, not from labor, for they had scarcely left their seats in the shuttle, but from peering through the gloom for some movement, some sign of the missing biologists.

Harkins sensed the fatigue in his crew, yet he decided to obey his schedule and keep pushing until songtide. They could rest for the hour or so while the trees bellowed and whistled and caterwauled, let them bathe if they did not mind the scummy waters, then the search could be resumed. He checked his watch. The Earth dial told him it would be ten in the

> morning back at the station. Here it was nearly dusk, less than half an hour until song- tide.
>
> "Movement there!" a voice cried suddenly.
>
> – *The Land Where Songtrees Grow*, Scott Sanders, **F&SF**, Sept. 1982, p. 5.

Here it is with Content Pattern tags inserted:

> **<Ongoing Activity>** Nothing moved except the searchers. **<Visuals>** In their shuttle they glided through the drowned forest, slipping over mats of waterplants, around hummocks smothered in ferns, beneath the arching roots of songtrees. Vines looped from branch to branch, gnarled ropes of purple, like crude decorations that no one had bothered to take down. Far overhead the canopy of purple leaves formed a continuous lacework roof, admitting daylight in slivers of lavender.
>
> The still waters divided at the prow of the shuttle, gathered again at the stern, and in a moment were still again. The eyes of the searchers ached. Their throats gagged on the steamy air. **<Backfill>** In only three days of hunting through the

> watery labyrinths of this vegetable planet they had grown weary, not from labor, for they had scarcely left their seats in the shuttle, but from peering through the gloom for some movement, some sign of the missing biologists.
>
> **<<Begin Scene** Harkins sensed the fatigue in his crew, yet he decided to obey his schedule and keep pushing until song-tide. They could rest for the hour or so while the trees bellowed and whistled and caterwauled, let them bathe if they did not mind the scummy waters, then the search could be resumed. He checked his watch. The Earth dial told him it would be ten in the morning back at the station. Here it was nearly dusk, less than half an hour until song- tide.
>
> **(Change Event)** "Movement there!" a voice cried suddenly.
>
> – *The Land Where Songtrees Grow*, Scott Sanders, **F&SF**, Sept. 1982, p. 5.

Here's the next example:

> I walked with my mother on Bodmin Moor.

The Moor is a large, wild area to the north-east of the county of Cornwall, England. Granite peaks push through the crumpled green land, on which are scattered ancient round stone huts.

That day, the sky was a lid of grey cloud.

We'd been talking about the Beast of Bodmin. The local papers—and sometimes the nationals—still report sightings of the Beast. For instance, there had been a recent case of a farmer in Simonsbath who said he lost a dozen lambs.

My mother snorted. "Ridiculous. Fifty miles away. Just locals trying it on. There can't have been any authentic sightings since—"

"Since when?"

"Well, around 1870."

And I knew then why I'd been summoned home. For the first time in my life, my mother was going to open up about the big family secret: the "thing in the barn" the fire—long before I was born—that killed my great-grandfather...and maybe something else.

—*Behold Now Behemoth*, Stephen Baxter, **Asimov's**, January 2000, p. 40.

And again with Content Pattern tags:

<Ongoing Activity> I walked with my mother on Bodmin Moor.

<Visuals> The Moor is a large, wild area to the north-east of the county of Cornwall, England. Granite peaks push through the crumpled green land, on which are scattered ancient round stone huts.

That day, the sky was a lid of grey cloud.

<Backfill> We'd been talking about the Beast of Bodmin. The local papers—and sometimes the nationals—still report sightings of the Beast. For instance, there had been a recent case of a farmer in Simonsbath who said he lost a dozen lambs.

<<Begin Scene My mother snorted. "Ridiculous. Fifty miles away. Just locals trying it on. There can't have been any authentic sightings since—"

"Since when?"

"Well, around 1870."

(Change Event) And I knew then why I'd been summoned home. For the first time in my life, my mother was going to open up about the big family secret: the

> "thing in the barn" the fire—long before I was born—that killed my great-grandfather...and maybe something else.
>
> —*Behold Now Behemoth*, Stephen Baxter, **Asimov's**, January 2000, p. 40.

ESSAY MODE

Essay mode is a <Thesis> followed by <Elaboration and concrete detail.>

Essay modes in openings tend to have:

1. High Abstraction nouns in either the Subject, the Predicate, or both, The combinations of sentences thus are:

<High Abstraction Subject & Concrete Predicate>

<Concrete Subject & High Abstraction Predicate>

<High Abstraction Subject & High Abstraction Predicate>

A second tendency is essay modes is the time-span covered by the thesis statement

2. the time span generally encompasses either many years, or is "timeless."

The time-span can be implicitly over the span of a character's adult life, to decades to millennia, or it can be "timeless," as in the fairy tale "Once upon a time."

From David Brin's *Startide Rising,* we have the following content pattern:

<Thesis = High Abstraction Subject & High Abstraction Predicate; time-span = thousands of years)>

> **<Thesis>** Fins had been making wisecracks about human beings for thousands of years. **<Elaboration>** They had *always* found men terribly funny. The fact that humanity had meddled in their genes and taught them engineering hadn't done much to change their attitude.
>
> Fins were smart-alecks.

– *Startide Rising,* David Brin, 1983, Bantam, p. 15.

<Thesis = High Abstraction Subject & High Abstraction Predicate; time-span = tens of thousands of years>

<Thesis> Mazes may be more ancient than mankind. **<Elaboration>** Certainly the cavemen constructed them by laying down football-sized stones, and perhaps by other means as well, now lost to us; the hill- forts of neolithic Europe were guarded by tangled dry ditches. Theseus followed a clue – a ball of thread – through the baffling palace of Minos, thus becoming the first in what threatens to be an infinited series of fictional detectives. The Fayre Rosamund dropped her embroidery with her needle thrust through it, but forgot the yarn in her pocket, thus furnishing Queen Eleanor's knights with the clue they required to solve Hampton Court Maze.

– *A Solar Labyrinth,* Gene Wolfe, **F&SF**, Apr., 1983, p. 50.

<Thesis = High Abstraction Subject & High Abstraction Predicate; time-span = null time>

> **<Thesis>** Take any repeated similar events—traffic accidents, stock transactions, baseball games—count and categorize them, and you get trends. **<Elaboration>** Trends in nature don't run without limit; the hitter who is improving doesn't eventually bat one thousand, the rising stock does not become worth more than the GNP, every car on the road doesn't hit every other one. Every trend reverses—watch long enough, and there's a pattern to the reversals. . . and where a lot of things reverse all at once, there's a cusp.
>
> – *Stochasm*, John Barnes, **Asimov's**, Nov. 1986, p.108.

Here's a few more short examples of theses:

<Thesis= High Abstraction Subject & Concrete Predicate; time span = decades>

> The villagers of Little Hangleton still called it "the Riddle House," even though

> it had been many years since the Riddle family had lived there.
>
> —*Harry Potter and the Goblet of Fire*, J.K. Rowling, p. 1, Scholastic Press, 2000.

<Thesis = Concrete Subject & High Abstraction Predicate; time-span encompasses adult life of the character>

> Joseph is a smart man, and a sullen man, and skeptical.
>
> —*Nodaway*, Robert Reed, **Asimov's**, Sept. 1999, p.16.

<Thesis = High Abstraction Subject & Concrete Predicate; time span = indeterminate>

> Human beings call me Mustardseed. As satellites of Uranus go,I wasn't much—barely three kilometers in radius compared to Titania's five hundred or so.
>
> —*Mustardseed*, G. David Nordley, **Asimov's**, Sept. 1999, p. 100.

<Thesis = High Abstraction Subject & Concrete Predicate, time-span is "time-less.">

> There was a girl named Helwar Ahl.
>
> – *Dapple: A Hwarath Romance,* Eleanor Arnason, **Asimov's**, Sept. 1999, p. 104.

<Concrete Subject & High Abstraction predicate, time span= the character's lives up to the moment the story begins)>

> Mr. and Mrs. Dursley of Number Four Privet Drive were proud to say that they were perfectly normal, thank you very much.
>
> – *Harry Potter and the Sorcerer's Stone,* J.K. Rowling, p. 1, 1997, Scholastic Press.

OTHER REASONS FOR TELLING IN THE OPENING

- The Focal character can't be identified with
- Information needs to be hidden from the reader
- The opening change event scene is too complex or too boring

Few people would say that a mature Theodore Sturgeon didn't know his craft. Many people don't know Sturgeon wrote some westerns, so here are some examples from *Sturgeon's West*.

In "Cactus Dance," Sturgeon has a botanist, Fortley Grantham, who "goes native" with peyote and comes to some odd conclusions. The change event is that Grantham has spent almost a year in the field, has sent a few letters, but no one has any idea if he's ever going to return to the college. This is hardly gripping drama. Second, Grantham, since he's stating some peculiar things under the influence of peyote, may in fact be insane, and no reader wants to be around a nutcase for an entire story. At the end, the narrator of the story feels Grantham has lost his mind, but the reader may have come to a different conclusion. Thus the story opens with a huge amount of telling:

> The book, they decided, would bring Fortley Grantham back East if nothing else would, and at first I'd agreed with them. Later, I didn't know. Later still, I hardly cared, for it grew heavy in my pack. Once, somewhere in the desert between Picacho and Vekol, two prospectors found me squatted on the scorching sand, heat-mad, dreaming out loud. It wouldn't do for them to explain to me about the puncture in my canteen; I insisted that the book had soaked up my water as I walked, and I could get it back by wringing it out. I still have the book, and on it still are my teethmarks.
>
> By train and stage and horse and mule I went, and, when I had to, on foot. I cursed the Territories in general and Arizona in particular. I cursed Prescott and Phoenix and Maricopa; Sacaton on the Gila River Reservation and Snowflake on Silver Creek. At Brownell in the Quijotas I learned that William Howard Taft had signed the enabling act that would make a state of that hellish country, and thereafter I cursed him too. From time to time I

even cursed myself and the stubborn streak which ran counter to comfort and career and intelligence itself—it would have been so simple, so wise, to go back to the green lawns of the Institute, the tinkle of teacups, to soft polite laughter and the coolness of ivied libraries.

But most of all—from his books to his beard, from his scalp to his scholarship—I cursed Fortley Grantham, who had leaped from the envied position of the Pudley Chair in Botany into this dehydrated wilderness. He could have died under the wheels of a brewery-dray, and I'd have wept and honored him. He might have risen to be Dean, perhaps even to Chairman. Failing these things, if he felt he must immolate himself in this special pocket of Hell, why could he not resign?

But no, not Fortley Grantham. He simply stayed out West, drifting, faintly radiating rumors that he was alive. If mail ever reached him, he never answered it. If he intended to return, he informed no one. He would not come back, he would not be decently dead, he would not resign.

And I wanted that Chair! I had worked for it. I had earned it. What was I to do—wait for some sort of Enoch Arden divorce between Grantham and the Chair, so that he would be legally dead and the Chair legally vacant? No, I must find him or his grave, bring him back or prove him dead.

His last letter had come from Silver King, and at Silver King they told me he'd gone to Florence. He had not, and I was tired and sick when I got there to learn that. A Mohave up from Arizona had seen him, though, and from there the trail led along the Union Pacific to Red Rock and then to the railhead at Silverbell.

Had it not been for a man of the cloth at Silverbell, a Reverend Sightly, I'd have lost the trail altogether. But the good man told me with horror in his voice, of the orgies indulged in by the local Indians, who sat in a ring around a fire gobbling mescal buttons and having visions. I took the trouble to correct the fellow as to the source of the narcotic, which comes from the peyotl and not from the mescal at all, whereupon he grew positively angry with me—not, as I first supposed, because I had found him in error, but because he took me to be "that unholy scoundrel who has brought the gifts of science to aid and abet the ignorant savage in his degraded viciousness."

When at last I convinced the reverend of the innocence of my presence and person, he apologized and explained to me that a renegade botanist was loose in the desert, finding the rare and fabled peyotl with unheard-of accuracy, and trading the beastly stuff to whoever wanted it.

From that point on the trail was long and winding, but at least it was clear. When I could, I inquired after Grantham, and when no one had heard of Grantham I had merely to ask about the problem of obtaining mescal buttons. Always there were stories of the white man who was not a prospector nor a miner nor a drummer nor anything else but the purveyor of peyotl. He was a tall, broad man with a red-and-silver beard and a way of cocking his head to one side a bit when he spoke. That was Grantham, all right—may the vultures gulp his eyeballs and die of it .

Between the Eagle Tails and Castle Dome is the head of Posas Valley, and at its head is a filthy little oasis called Kofa. I confess I was happy to see it. It was August, and the heat and the glare had put knobs like knuckles in my sinus tissues; I could feel them grind together as I breathed.

I was afoot, the spavined nag I had bought in Arlington having died in New Water Pass. I had a burro for my pack and gear, and it was all she could handle. She was old and purblind, and if she had left her strength and durability behind with her youth, she had at least left her stubbornness too. She carried the little she could and let me walk.

I could hardly have been more depressed. I had little money left, and less hope. My canteen was a quarter-full of tepid mud which smelled faintly of the dead horned toad I'd seen in the waterhole in the pass. My feet hurt and my hipjoints creaked audibly as I plodded along. Half silently I mumbled what I once facetiously had called my "Anthem for Grantham," a sort of chant which ran:

...I shall people his classroom with morons. I shall have him seduced by his chambermaid and I shall report it to the Dean. I shall publicly refute his contention that the Echinopsis cacti are separate from the genus Cereus. I shall lock him in his rooms at banquet time on Founder's Day. I shall uproot his windowboxes and spread rumors about him with the Alumni Association

It was the only way I had left of cheering myself up.

For weeks I had trailed the rumors of Grantham's peyotl traffic farther and farther from peyotl grounds. It was sahuro country here, and all about they stretched their yearning, other-worldly arms out and upward, as if in search for a lover who might forget their thorns. Down the valley, westward, was a veritable forest of Dracenoideae, called yucca hereabouts. I did not know if yucca and peyotl could coexist, and I thought not. If not, my main method of trailing Grantham was lost.

In such hopeless depression I staggered into Kofa, which, primitive as it was, afforded a chance of better company than my black thoughts and a doddering burro. I knew better than to hope for a restaurant and so went to the sole source of refreshment, the bar.

It seemed so dark inside, after the merciless radiance outside, that I stood blinking like an owl for thirty seconds before I could orient myself. At last I could locate the bar and deduce that a man stood behind it.

I croaked out an order for a glass of milk, which the bar tender greeted with a thundering laugh and the quotation of a price so fantastic that I was forced to order whiskey, which I despise. The fool's nostrils spread when I demanded water with the whiskey, but he said nothing as he poured it from a stone jar.

I took the two glasses as far back in that 'dobe cavern as I could get from him, and slumped down into a chair. For a long moment there was nothing in my universe but the feel of my lips in the water, which, though alkaline, was wet and cool.

<BEGIN SCENE>

Only then, leaning back and breathing deeply, did I realize that someone sat across the table from me. He cocked his head on one side and said, "Well, well! If Mahomet won't come to the mountain, the Institute brings forth a mouse."

"Dr. Grantham!"

– *Cactus Dance,* Theodore Sturgeon, "Sturgeon's West," p. 49-53, Doubleday, 1973.

In *The Man Who Figured Everything*, the POV character is an undercover Marshal. The problem is, Sturgeon wants this info hidden from the reader until mid-way into the story.

> This is about Jim Conlin the Badlands Bookkeeper. He was, according to the journals of the time, a terror, a menace, and a scourge. He was, in the flesh, a mild man, young and balding early, with diffident horizontal lines across his brow.
>
> He hid in the hills with his half-dozen riders, all but one of whom outweighed him, but then that one was only a three-quarter breed Nez Percé, and hardly counted. These men, each to his taste, fought and gambled, drank and wenched, always providing they had Jim Conlin's advance permission and pursued the hobby somewhere away from Jim Conlin's hideout. A long way away. There was a town, Dead Mole Spring, eight miles away as the crow flies, where nobody had ever seen Conlin or any of his crew—a good example of the way the Bookkeeper of the Badlands arranged things.
>
> Jim Conlin figured. He figured everything, the Bookkeeper did. He never

moved until he was ready, and when he was ready, it was altogether. In some sleepy mountain town, just when the marshal was out and the sheriff drunk, and the bank heavy with cowpokes' pay and prospectors' dust, Jim Conlin's men would whirl up out of the ground like dust devils and be gone like smoke, the gold with them.

The only similarity between one job and another was that element of perfect planning, perfect timing—the only clue, most of the time, as to who the robbers were. Unless, of course, Conlin wanted it otherwise, like the time he took the Rocky Summit Bank three times in one week, just because everybody was so positive he wouldn't be back.

He would have been caught for sure the time rumors got around that he was going to rob the express between Elwood and Casson's Quarry; the train was loaded with law and the tracks lined on both sides with one of the biggest posses the West had ever seen, which was fine with Conlin, who was busy at the time robbing another train on another railroad.

He would certainly be remembered in large type, like Butch Cassidy and the James boys, if it were not for his concentration on fine detail—this got him only into fine print. As a man, he was colorless to the point of invisibility; as a desperado he was too methodical to be remembered. Probably the largest two reasons his reputation has faded with the newspapers of his day were these: he never killed a lawman, and he was never caught.

There came one night to Jim Conlin's hideout, Arch Scott, invited and escorted. Scott had something of a reputation locally: cautious, sober, with special skills in safes and lockboxes. He could use a gun, and didn't, which was a high recommendation to the Bookkeeper; and Scott's ability to do nine consecutive jobs with the methods of nine different people clinched it.

Although the Bookkeeper occasionally took on a brace or two of drifters for special jobs, letting them go afterwards, he liked to keep a half-dozen regulars with him; and there was a vacancy just now, one Fancy Moore having succumbed to romance. (That was Conlin's name for it; actually it was tetanus, contracted after a Rocky Summit housewife, mistaken for a doxie by Moore, removed his ear with an iron skillet.)

So Conlin gave Arch Scott his guided tour and his most careful examination, introducing him around, watching him, making his estimate. He liked Scott—liked him, that is, the way a man likes a well-made saddle or a clean rifle. The Bookkeeper had human feelings, but he had a place for them, and he kept them all there. Which introduces Loretta Harper.

She was the only woman permitted at the hideout, except for a few squaws who washed clothes and swept out. Conlin had found her working in a place she was glad to get out of—especially with a man who knew enough about her to ask no questions and saw to it that she got more of the things she liked than she could hope for working in town. He had something for all her hungers but one, and that one was beyond his comprehension. It was beyond hers, too, until Arch Scott came.

"This here's Loretta," Conlin said when he brought Scott in, and Scott saw a carving come to life, silk and ivory and ice, as out of place here as a leaf from Godey's Lady's Book tacked to a haybarn; and Loretta saw a neat man with heavy shoulders and good teeth and eyes you couldn't keep secrets from.

And that should have been that. It would have been, as far as Arch was concerned. He was there on business, and business came first. And Loretta felt nothing, just then; Jim Conlin's men came and went and his steady crew was always there. This was another one, only another one. As Conlin and Scott left she turned back to her mirror, and if anyone had asked her, she probably wouldn't have remembered the new man's name.

Conlin and Arch Scott went down the mountain for fifty yards or so to the cabin and went in. "Henry Little Hawk," said Conlin, nodding at the slight figure squatting by the door.

<BEGIN SCENE>

"Howdy," said Scott. "I'm—"

"Yuh," grunted the little man. He looked like an animated piece of mahogany, and seemed to be composed mainly of eyebrows, nose, and sharp shinbones.

Conlin chuckled. "He knows who you are. He's the one found you for me...

> – *The Man Who Figured Everything,* Theodore Sturgeon and Don Ward, "Sturgeon's West," p.103-106. Doubleday, 1973.

In *Well Spiced* we again have a situation where information needs to be hidden from the reader (a wealthy speculator, Barstow, has created a new town to rival the town of Tamarisk. The purpose: to lure the railroad into going through *his* new town. However, the new town is built around a phony well, and it will be Pericles Zapappas' job to solve a "mystery:" how has Barstow found ample well water where no one—in all the years of Tamarisk's history—had ever found any before? We therefore need to know something about the town of Tamarisk and Pericles Zapappas.

> Tamarisk just happened. Some forgotten Conestoga cap'n had chosen the Tamarisk hollow as a route down the valley, rather than the exactly similar hollow on the other side of the rise. The town's first building appeared when one Pericles Zapappas sold the oxen which hauled his chuck wagon. The old wagon, hub-deep in the sandy soil, was the nucleus. Because it was there, it was logical to set up

a general supplies shack near it, and because of the shack and its increasing stock, settlers took to the nearby lush foothills, knowing they had a trading place. With the settlers came the helpers and the hangers-on, the blacksmiths and the gamblers, the assay office and the livery stable and the hotel.

Pericles Zapappas stuck with Tamarisk. He hadn't planned to; he hadn't planned not to. It was just that there were so many people to feed—and he liked feeding people. He liked to see the tin plates, and later, the thick china ones, mopped clean with great chunks of sourdough bread, or the muscular black loaves he baked himself. The old wagon soon sported a canvas awning which became a mess tent which gradually acquired wooden walls and a tin roof, and as the busy years and the busy wagon trains passed, there was a new building with a real kitchen, rows of iron skillets, three glass sugar bowls, and a spittoon.

Pericles was the only fixture that showed no change. He was a grizzled, tubby little man, with a complexion the color of a frankfurter and a skin like a silk pillow slip that has been slept on for three hot nights. His eyes were round, clear, and blue, giving the impression of red-hot portholes into an ice box. He smiled often, never laughed, and was always a little frightened—afraid that the meat wouldn't arrive, that the coffee would boil, that a customer wasn't getting enough to eat. He absorbed insults and compliments with the same gentle smile and the same shuffling backward retreat, as from royalty.

Tamarisk was good to live in, as such places go, when the wind was from the hills. But when it came panting up from the desert with fire and salt on its breath, the town shimmered and crackled and dried in it. It was on such a day that Fellows stamped into Pericles's place, and the youth's language was not one whit less blistering than the desert wind. His profanity swirled in, all but sweeping Pericles off his precarious perch on a serving table, where he was hanging mesh bags of garlic, strings of melon rind, and chains of herbs and barks to dry; for Pericles was a great hand in the spice department.

<BEGIN SCENE>

"Feed me!" roared Fellows. "By God, likker won't do fer this. Gimme some o'

> that slumgullion of yours, the kind that wallops you hot an' then smooths you off easy."

When Sturgeon has an opening that doesn't require a lot of background information, and nothing needs to be hidden, he opens with a scene:

> Delia Fox stood in the center of the saddle shed, her face pale, her thin lips sucked in and bitten on, invisible. The Circle F's steady rider, Vic Ryan, squatted on his tall heels with his back to the wall and laughed at her. "All right, all right—I'll raid, I'll gun out your nester." He laughed again. "But under orders." He aimed the stem of his pipe at her. "The boss's orders."
>
> "You know he'll never!"
>
> "If I raid, he will," said Ryan easily. "And he'll give me those orders right up to and includin' the minute I kick in that nester's shack door."
>
> "You mean you want him to go with you?"
>
> "That's about it."
>
> "That's the same thing as saying you won't go."

> Ryan shrugged and began to pack his pipe. "I reckon hell *could* freeze over."
>
> She stamped to the door. "Catch a lot of folks with some heavy hauling to do, the day it does," she snapped, and went out.
>
> – *The Waiting Thing Inside,* Theodore Sturgeon and Don Ward, "Sturgeon's West," p. 81. Doubleday, 1973.

If you look on her website, JK Rowling had several possible openings for *Harry Potter and the Sorcerer's Stone.* Originally, she had Voldemort killing Harry's family. But she eventually rejected this draft. Why? She doesn't say why, but let's think about this. First, Harry is only one year old, and doesn't make for a good focal character, since he would be barely verbal at this age. Second, the battle with Voldemort would have to be broken-up by exposition on wizard combat techniques. Third, it gives away crucial information on why Harry survived. Finally, Rowling can't do it from Voldemort's point of view, or the reader will be misled into thinking the novel is "Hannibal, with magic," however, if Rowling does the story from, say, Harry's mother's POV, then we have the situation of killing a focal character in a few pages.

Thus the first chapter of *Harry Potter and the Sorcerer's Stone* is separated into two sections. The first, dealing with Vernon Dursley's day, is almost all telling. The second takes place outside their house where Dumbledore and McGonagal talk. This latter section is all scenic. Why? Why was it handled this way? In the first place, Rowling doesn't want us to identify with Vernon Dursley. If it were handled scenically, the reader might jump to the conclusion that "This is a story about a nasty bourgeois conformist." Yet as we follow Dursley through his day, there are little "bits" that stand out—they are mini "scenes" taking place in real-time. Dursley sees a cat reading a map, sees people dressed weirdly, overhears the name "Harry Potter" mentioned by some of the weirdos at lunch. It's like we're seeing Vernon Dursley (thankfully) through a narrative overcast, but on every page "bright sunlight" in the form of mini-scenes breaks through a Vaseline-smeared lens.

The first real scene we have is when he asks his wife what exactly her nephew's name is. The next section of Chapter One, is almost all scene: Dumbledore dialogues with McGonagal, reveals that the Potters are dead, Voldemort's power is destroyed, and that Harry somehow mysteriously survived. Only the last few lines of Chapter One are telling.

OPENING WITH A SCENE

There *are* professional stories, of course, that begin with a scene. But it is instructive to note the common traits. In general, spec stories that begin scenically have the following in common:

- The character is quiescent physically, and generally, emotionally as well
- The setting is either mundane or a commonplace of the genre
- Change is either happening or imminent
- The "heart" of the story can be dramatized with few words

And Finally,

- The description of the speculative idea can be delayed until later without confusion

OR,

- The spec idea or "heart" of the story can be easily dramatized in the opening scene

There are a number of situations that allow for smoother exposition in a scene:

- The change event wakes up the character
- The character is quietly mulling or ruminative
- The character is engaged in a monotonous activity like commuting
- The character is waiting for another person

PART 2—HOOKING THE READER: PATTERNS IN PROFESSIONAL STORY OPENINGS

Introduction

Orson Scott Card states that there are three "don'ts" in fiction writing that are guaranteed to lose the reader. I must say that I have to agree. In my dim recollection, I've rejected fiction for three main reasons. Generally it was because I wound up saying one of the following things:

I'm confused
I don't care; why should I keep reading?
I don't believe it

How to Improve Your Speculative Fiction Openings was intended to help you avoid the problems of reader confusion. The reader reaction of, "I don't believe it," seems to be solved primarily by careful plotting.

In this section we'll deal with "hooks." What are the ways and means that pros use to interest the reader?

But first, why is this important to you? At the time I'm writing this, September of 2012, it seems to be becoming increasingly important.

Mickey Spillane had a proverb that I love. He said, "The first line sells your novel. The last line sells your *next* novel." Put in other terms, the first line starts building your relationship with the reader, the last line "seals" the relationship. Give them a memorable experience, and the reader may go online and look for other things you've written.

So hooking the reader is quite important. However, with electronic publishing shaking the print world to its foundations, *it now becomes ten times more important*.

Even as I write this, the editors of magazines and publishing houses are being by-passed by readers downloading ten thousand free titles into their e-readers.

In effect, the individual reader is a now a slush-pile reader, and you now have an opportunity to sell yourself *directly* to your potential reader.

Types of Reader Engagement

There are many ways to engage a reader. Here are three that I *won't* be examining. 1) a narrator whose "voice" is quite interesting, 2) humor, and, 3) highly polished prose.

I won't be dealing with these possibilities because, first, I question how much the creation of a great narrative voice or humor can be learned. Engaging narrators seem to be more the product of talent than study, and the same seems to hold true for humor. The supremely polished style is often the product of exhaustive re-writing (In the case of *Soldier of Fortune,* a story in the Best American Short Stories, 2011, author Bret Anthony Johnston states that he re-wrote it a dozen times.)

In examining the openings of pros we can find several loci or organizing patterns of engaging reader interest:

Death & Disaster
Stress / Social Stress
Speculative Idea - oddity
Curiosity

Death & Disaster

Among the possibilities in the Death & Disaster locus there are:

risk to life and limb
death

violence
war
physical conflict
disaster
illicit activity
suffering
imprisonment
surveillance

In Catalog A, I've compiled examples of Death & Disaster loci subcategorized by whether the hook information is foreshadowed, happening in the "present," or in the past, and also by specific opening technique. Opening techniques can involve the use of an epigram, or opening with dialogue, or "direct narration." Direct narration is what we see most of the time - the author just "starts the story" by addressing the reader; for example, "In a hole in the ground there lived a hobbit.")

In your own story, it would be worthwhile to consider whether any of the loci above occur in the past, present or future of your opening. If so, there's a possibility of using it to hook your reader through foreshadowing, or describing it in the present or past. I've placed these examples first because they're often recombined with Speculative Idea-Oddity, and it's often easier to spot Death & Disaster loci in your story.

Stress / Social Stress

Catalog B gives examples of Stress / Social Stress as hooks, again broken down by subcategory. Among the possibilities are:

conflict
social anxiety
stressful situations (in rare cases, it can be a positive stress, such as falling in love at first sight)

Speculative idea – oddity

More complex than the two loci above, Spec-idea-oddity involves finding some peculiarity or striking aspect of the spec-idea, and illustrating it in the opening. Often this involves combining it with the above two loci -- a double hook as it were. Catalog C will give examples of Spec-idea-oddity, along with some combined examples.

Curiosity

Something for more experienced or talented writers, Curiosity involves presenting peculiar strands of information to the reader in such a way that the reader says, "What the *heck* is going on here?" Catalog D gives some examples of Curiosity as a hook.

Descriptive Statistics

I have a four-inch stack of openings, and have broken them out according to the subcategories. Bear in mind, some of these combine types. Here are rough the percentages:

Speculative idea-oddity - 39%
Disaster & Death - 19%
Curiosity - 19%
Stress / Social Stress - 18%
Unclassified - 5%

How to use the Catalogs

It's my hope that by studying the various openings as categories, you can start to "absorb" the loci and start seeing the hook possibilities in your own works.

CATALOGS

As with the prior section, I'm giving you a bunch of examples. I've subcategorized these openings in a way that I hope is helpful. I've also numbered the examples "1 of 5," "2 of 5," for ease in flipping through them.

CATALOG A, Death & Disaster

As an author it might be fruitful to see if any of the following Death & Disaster subcategories occur in your story:

risk to life and limb
death
violence
war
physical conflict
disaster
illicit activity
suffering
imprisonment
surveillance

Do these subcategories happen before, or after, the planned opening of your story? Here are examples.

Death & Disaster

1 of 21

"Somebody shot and killed Dr. Bennett behind the Food Mart on April Street!" Ceci Moore says breathlessly as I take the washing off the line.

I stand with a pair of Jack's boxer shorts in my hand and stare at her. I don't like Ceci. Her smirking pushiness, her need to shove her scrawny body into the middle of every situation, even ones she'd be better off leaving alone. She'd been that way ever since high school. But we were neighbors; we're stuck with each other. Dr. Bennett delivered both Shawn and Jackie. Slowly I fold the boxer shorts and lay them in my clothes basket...

---*Evolution*, Nancy Kress, Asimov's, Oct. 1995, p. 21.

< dialogue opening, death in the past >

2 of 21

"Keep as far away as you can," Doc Burner warned when he looked up from the body on the motel bed.

Jake Lucas backed against the door of the room, wishing the dead man's toy poodle would stop making that noise. As Sheriff he'd faced bikers on PCP, drunks the size of sumo wrestlers, even gentle wife killers, but never a whining poodle. "Just what's wrong, Doc?"…

---*The Man in the Dinosaur Coat*, John Alfred Taylor, Asimov's, July 1994, p. 82.

< dialogue opening, death in the past >

3 of 21

"No," Sarah's mother said, her voice barely more than a whisper around the tubes. "You can't. They kill people in there."

Sarah held her mother's good hand—the one without the IV. Small chips dotted her mother's face and body, each scanning vital signs. It made her look as if she had chickenpox…

---*Reflections on Life and Death,* Kristine Kathryn Rusch, Asimov's, Jan. 1998, p. 34.

< dialogue opening, death foreshadowed >

4 of 21

I suppose I can just keep talking until the oxygen runs out.

Yes, that would be a good idea, wouldn't it? Because then it'll be an anaerobic environment in here and no bacteria will grow. I'll be in better shape when they find me. Less effort for the one who has to piece together what happened…and less upsetting for Nan. I mustn't forget that!...

---*Black Smoker,* Kage Baker, Asimov's, Jan. 2000, p. 48.

< direct-narrative opening, disaster foreshadowed >

5 of 21

The bent old man watched the two thugs enter the ruins of the warehouse.

Between them they strutted fifty kilos of surgically-implanted muscles…

---*Not Worth a Cent,* R. Neube, Asimov's, April/May 2006, p. 158.

< direct-narrative opening, "risk to life & limb" foreshadowed >

6 of 21

The dream came again, once more full of greens and reds and children's faces. They were ugly, teasing, taunting, hating faces. They were beautiful peaches-and-cream, laughing, shouting, joyous faces.

Fria opened her eyes with a start, frightened to discover that she had not been sleeping after all. She shivered at the realization. The doctors of so long ago had warned that hallucinations would be the first sign of the impending end, the first evidence that all of humankind is mortal. Nothing is forever…

---*Who Will Guard the Guardians?* Catherine McCollum and Michael McCollum, Oct. 1982, p. 150.

< direct-narrative opening, disaster foreshadowed >

7 of 21

The weight of the gun in his pocket pulled down the right side of his windbreaker. No matter how often Jack shrugged, he still felt uncomfortable. It was as if someone behind him was resting a hand on his shoulder. The walk down to the river would have been pleasant on another day. The sun had just set, and the summer heat was already slipping out of the air. The trees that lined the river were still green, but less brilliant than they had been just a couple of weeks before…

---*Jaycee,* Daniel Abraham, Asimov's, Dec. 1999, p. 50.

< direct-narrative opening, violence foreshadowed >

8 of 21

Tan says they intend to give us all some kind of painful disease. He claims he overheard them talking about it when they brought him here. I don't know whether to believe him or not.

"Will it be fatal, do you think?" one of the others asks---Ani, the female next to me. "Will we die?"...

---*The Scientific Community,* Lois Tilton, Asimov's, Sept. 1999, p. 40.

< direct-narrative opening, suffering foreshadowed >

9 of 21

On the eve of destruction we had oysters and champagne.

Don't suppose for a moment that we had any desire to lord it over the poor mortals of San Francisco, in that month of April, in that year of 1906; but things weren't going to be so gracious there again for a long while, and we felt an urge to fortify ourselves against the work we were to do.

And who were *we* you might ask? The present-time operatives of Dr. Zeus Incorporated, a twenty-fourth century cabal of investors who have presided...

---*Son Observe the Time,* Kage Baker, Asimov's, May 1999, p. 94.

< direct-narrative opening, disaster foreshadowed >

10 of 21

I come from the Middle West, and unforgiving land with little or no tolerance for imagination. The wind blows harsh across the prairies, and the snows fall thick. Even with the convenience of the modern age, life is dangerous there. Two lose sight of reality, even for one short romantic moment, is to risk death.

I didn't belong in that country, and my grandfather knew it. I was his namesake, and somehow, being the second Nick Carraway in a family where the name had a certain mystique had forced that mystique upon me...

---*The Beautiful, the Damned,* Kristine Kathryn Rusch, F&SF, Feb. 1995, p. 36.

< direct-narrative opening, disaster foreshadowed >

11 of 21

Breathing is a reflex, but taking control of your breathing demands conscious effort, especially since the bellows of the lung is where your legs used to be. You blink your eyes, then feebly lift your arm to dab them clear before you ask "What's that date?"

"October 8, 1998."

Almost three years since the last time they needed your expertise. "Bosnia again?"

"Naw, a place called Kosovo."...

---*Calamity of so Long Life*, John Alfred Taylor, Asimov's, May 2000, p. 62.

< direct-narrative opening, war foreshadowed >

12 of 21

Keeping a tail on the taxi ahead of me was the easy part. Staying discreet about it wasn't. The white taxi and my Audi were the only two vehicles on a gravel road, and the twin rooster tails of dust rose at least ten yards into the cloudless sky. I did my best....

---*In the Shade*, Edward Bryant, F&SF, Oct. 1982, p. 77.

< direct-narrative opening , surveillance, in the present >

13 of 21

WE REACH HIM TOO LATE, pulling him out of the curing pond, nothing left but a melted body and a pain-twisted face. For a moment or two, we talk about the dead expeditor, how he was good and why he wasn't perfect, and why he killed himself—because he was imperfect, but noble is why…

---*Due*, Robert Reed, F&SF, Feb. 2000, p. 121.

< direct-narrative opening, death in the past >

14 of 21

WE FOUND THE POOR OLD guy lying in garbage and quite a lot of his own blood in the alley next to the Midnight Mission. His shoes had been stolen -- no way of knowing if he'd been wearing socks -- and whatever had been in the empty, dirty paper bag he was clutching. But his fingernails were immaculate, and he had no beard stubble. Maybe sixty, maybe older. No way of telling at a cold appraisal.

There were three young women down on their knees, weeping and flailing toward the darkening sky. It was going to rain, a brick-mean rain. Bag ladies in an alley like that, yeah, no big surprise...but these weren't gap toothed scraggy harridans. I recognized two of them from commercials; I think the precise term is *supermodel.* Their voices outshone the traffic hissing past the alley mouth. They were obviously very broken up at the demise of this old bum…

---*Objects of Desire in the Mirror are Closer Than They Appear*, Harlan Ellison, F&SF, Oct./Nov. 1999, p. 75.

< direct-narrative opening, violence in the past, stress in the present >

15 of 21

It was an accident, really, an accident so improbable as to be within a hair's breadth of impossible. Yet, every individual human life is the sum of similar vast improbabilities, so the accident may have had a certain cosmic inevitability about it. I don't know. I drive ships for a living, and leave big questions to the priests, philosophers, and physicists.

My chief engineer, Val Steiner, triggered this particular accident...

---*Odysseus*, John G. Hemry, Analog, Feb. 1999, p. 72.

< direct-narrative opening, disaster in the past >

16 of 21

The sun crawled steadily up behind the dying city. Its rays stretched across towers and avenues to the hillside, through the window of a shack, to the eyelids of six-year-old 'jum. The sunbeams teased 'jum to wake up and look out upon Reyo City, and count the many lightcraft rising to meet the ship's in orbit around L'li...

---*The Children Star,* Analog, April 1998, p.12.

< direct-narrative opening, disaster in the present (dying city) >

17 of 21

Being part of a legend is okay, after the fact, but, as I look back on what we belters have come to know as "The Battle of Alice's Asteroid," I wouldn't recommend the process to anyone. I paid for my fame, not just with wounds and suffering, but, in the end, with my heart twice over. Times are changing now, thanks in part to Alice, and it has come time to take care of some unfinished business; they say confession is good for the soul. Especially when you might be forgiven…

---*Alice's Asteroid,* G. David Nordley, Asimov's, Oct. 1995, p. 64.

< direct-narrative opening, war in past >

I WASN'T SNOOPING. I'VE read all the advice books and know that children need their privacy. But Tommy had been using the car the night before, and my keys were nowhere to be found, so I looked in his room.

Unlike the stereotypical teenage boy, Tommy keeps his room fairly neat. Oh, the bed was unmade, but there wasn't any dirty laundry on the floor or used dishes on the desk. A quick glance showed that the keys weren't on his bedside table or the dresser.

I started looking in drawers. Perhaps he had put them away without thinking. The top dresser drawer held nothing but socks, and the desk drawer had been missing ever since my husband bought the thing for his first apartment. That left the bedside table.

The bedside table held a stack of magazines (two copies of Rolling Stone covering up a Sports Illustrated swimsuit issue and a Penthouse; maybe I was snooping just a little), the microphone from an old cassette recorder, a box of colored pencils, some pennies, and a matchbox. Inside the matchbox were nine little green triangular pills. I knew exactly what they were too. Efracol. The seduction pill.

After all, I'd invented it...

---*A Diagram of Rapture,* James L. Cambias, F&SF, April 2000, p. 78.

< direct-narrative opening, illicit activity in the past >

19 of 21

Dusk is the best time to steal, out here in the bay. You'd think dark would be safer, but that isn't so. At night, people go on the alert. They listen when their watch-dogs bark, and the shackboats are full of watchdogs. They grab for guns. At dusk the day-jobbers and are coming home, tired from chipping ice on the bergs, working the pier shops, or the flea-markets...

---*Rat,* Mary Rosenblum, Asimov's, Oct. 1994, p. 66.

< direct-narrative opening, illicit activity foreshadowed >

20 of 21

How many shapes of pain are there?
Are any topologically equivalent?
And is one of them death?

BIANTHA WOKE TO A HEAVY knocking on the door and found her face pressed against a book's musty pages…

---*Counting Shapes,* Yoon Ha Lee, F&SF, June 2001, p. 4.

< epigram opening of suffering and death, followed by stress in the present >

21 of 21

When the stars threw down their spears
And water'd heaven with their tears:

---William Blake

All I wanted was a safe landing. Our frightening, turbulent descent dropped us through towering anvils of lightning-wracked storm clouds that shook and shoved our huge landing shuttle with violent bursts of wind as we dropped below sixty thousand feet and headed into our approach to Caledonia's sole landing strip…

---*To Leuchars*, Rick Wilbur, Asimov's, Sept. 2000, p. 50.

< epigram opening of suffering, followed by threat to life & limb, in the present >

CATALOG B, Stress / Social Stress

1 of 8

The lunar lander descended onto the dusty pad, the fading blue cross and on its side -- the Blue Moon resorts logo -- lost in the rising dust. As the lander touched the pad, it yawed unsteadily before bumping gently back down.

Please, I prayed, *no glitches*. I looked at my watch: the media conference was scheduled to begin in 2 hours…

--- *Name That Moon*, Robert Onopa, F&SF, Jan. 2001, p.137.

< direct-narrative opening, stress in the present and foreshadowed >

2 of 8

"Eyes to front, Dupree!" The drill commander barked. "You will get no special consideration here, human." His fangs flashed as he tapped his open four-fingered hand rhythmically with the short, spike-covered training baton used to 'encourage' lazy cadets. The unspoken derisive 'female' was equally clear.

My eyes snapped back to the four-legged bulk of the cadet in front of me on the large grass exercise area behind the barracks...

---*Trade Warriors*, F. Alexander Brejcha, Analog, Oct. 1998, p.10.

< dialogue opening, social stress in the present >

3 of 8

"The invaders have been on Kya *three months*," the man said angrily. He seemed ready to jump out of the screen and pound on Delores Jones's desk. "*Three months*. The Kya can't stop them. When is the U.N. going to *fight*?"

"I'm sorry, sir." Delores struggled to sound pleasant and sincere in the face of the businessman's wrath. You'd think he was here on Kya, she mused, not safely back on Earth. "I can't discuss the war."...

---*Roundup*, W.R. Thompson, Analog, Sept. 1998, p. 10.

< dialogue opening, social stress in the present >

4 of 8

The supervisor's door opened itself at my approach. Nguyen Duc Pho looked up, and immediately saw something he disliked. "You don't seem happy to be here, Dar."

I shouldn't have let my annoyance show. He could contact me in my work-booth, but he loves face-to-face meetings. I softened my visage, despite his using that nickname I hate.

"Just a feeling it's bad news, sir." Police work rarely gives one good news...

---*Live Bait*, Shane Tourtellotte, Analog, July/August 1999, p. 116.

< direct-narrative opening, social stress in the present, and foreshadowed >

5 of 8

"This is a bad idea, Susan."

Susan Wrigley ignored her sister's warning, hastening her tottery gait down the bright hospital corridor…

---*Image of an Imperfect God,* Shane Tourtellotte, Analog, March 1999, p. 96.

< dialogue opening, stress foreshadowed >

6 of 8

"NOT GUILTY!" CRIED THE foreman of the jury that day in 1989, and the courtroom in the New Orleans federal court "erupted in pandemonium," as next morning's *Times-Picayune* expressed it.

My lawyer, who had been nervously fingering some documents, tossed his papers into the air and embraced me…

---*The Great Ancestor,* Albert E. Cowdrey, F&SF, Sept. 1998, p.57.

< dialogue opening, positive stress >

7 of 8

STUCK IN THE PRINCIPAL'S office for not listening again. He had to be the only kid who regularly got sent there for not doing anything…

---*Fighting Gravity,* Laurel Winter, F&SF, Sept. 1998, p. 132.

< narrative opening, stress in the present >

8 of 8

The Town Council meeting was split down the middle – the Hullabaloo colonists on the one side and Fenella Elane Tyne on the other. Jerram stood in the back and admired the way Fenella strove to convince the tired farmers. Pacing around the podium, she brought to bear the power of her unmatched intelligence, impeccable honesty, and polished verbal skills. In the discordant discussion that followed, Jerram studied her serious face. She was magnificent, but hopelessness

> coursed through him. She didn't have a chance of winning anyone over to her side. And he didn't stand a chance of winning her…
>
> ---*Hullabaloo,* Diane Turnshek, Analog, July/Aug. 2000, p. 203.
>
> < narrative opening, stress in the present and foreshadowed >

CATALOG C

Speculative idea-oddity

This technique involves dramatizing the speculative idea in some vivid or striking way. Often, this category uses backfill or a change event in the opening.

1 of 16

> The reeling flicker of days slowed, steadied, froze. A quick look around. The time machine was sitting on grass. Beyond the grass: buildings. It was, recognizably, Central Park. Manhattan. With a huge sigh of relief -- so far, no nuclear war -- Jack Fabrax dismounted, clambering down onto the grass, lugging

> the heavy suitcase after him. God, what a weight! The time machine flickered and dissolved. It would return in precisely seventy-two hours…
>
> ---*Heroes of the Third Millennium*, Hugh Cook, F&SF, Dec. 1998, p. 99.
>
> < change event focused >

2 of 16

> TOWARD THE END OF THE meeting, the caseworker remarked, "Oh -- and one more thing. Dennis thinks he's a Martian."
>
> "I beg your pardon?" I wasn't certain I had heard correctly. I had papers scattered all over the meeting room table -- thick piles of stapled incident reports, manila-foldered psychiatric evaluations, Xeroxed clinical diagnoses, scribbled caseworker histories, typed abuse reports, bound trial transcripts, and my own crabbed notes as well: Hyperactivity. Fetal Alcohol Syndrome. Emotional Abuse. Physical Abuse. Conners Rating Scale. Apgars. I had no idea there was so much to know about children. For a moment, I

was actually looking at a folder labeled *Martian.*

"He thinks he's a Martian," Ms. Bright repeated. She was a small woman, very proper and polite. "He told his group home parents that he's not like the other children -- he's from Mars -- so he shouldn't be expected to act like an Earthling all the time."...

---*The Martian Child,* David Gerrold, F&SF, Sept. 1995, p. 124.

< change event focused, combined with curiosity >

3 of 16

"WOMEN! WORRIED? TIRED? Frustrated? At a Dead End? Ready for excitement of a new and different kind? Send your picture and a brief biography to our catalog. We'll connect you with someone who can take care of all your needs!"

Sally brushed sweaty bangs off her forehead and blinked a few times to clear her eyes. All around her, dryers and washing machines whirled, chugged, and rattled. The air was full of the clashing scents of different fabric softeners. By the Launderland door, silhouetted against the blazing day outside, two children wrestled over a toy truck and snarled at each other…

---*A Choice of Graces,* Robin Aurelian, F&SF, Mar. 1999, p. 42.

< change event focused, combined with stress in the present >

4 of 16

THE FIRST TIME I MET SKY Eyes, I thought she was blind. Her eyes were clouded white-blue, with no black circles in the middle, no white background. I thought she was blind, and then she looked at me and saw that I was seven years old and my mother was sick with something that ate her until her arms were brown sticks and my father wouldn't admit it and I wanted everything to be back the way it was, but knew -- even then -- that it could never be that way again.

I don't know how I knew this, but I did…

---*Sky Eyes*, Laurel Winter, F&SF, Mar. 1999, p. 54.

< backfill, combined with disaster and suffering in the past >

5 of 16

"Now look, Bobby," the alien said. "If you promise not to tell anybody about this, we can do a lot of neat stuff for you."

"You don't have to talk down to me," Bobby said. "I'm almost eight." Bobby tried hard to look right at the alien's eyes and not let him know how scared he was. The alien looked just like anybody else, except for a weird greenish glow around him, kind of like an oil slick. His *aura*, the alien called it.

"I'm sorry," the alien said. "But it's true. We can do a lot for you."

"Like what?"

"Clothes. Your own TV. Stuff like that. What do you want?"...

---*Promises*, Lewis Shiner, F&SF, Dec. 1982, p. 32.

< change event focused >

Exhausted, Jessup sees the change as it happens this time. On page 1548 of *The Experience of Literature*, 3rd ed., in the chronological listing of the works of Ernest Hemingway, the title *The Old Man and the Sea* materializes in crisp, black letters. Other words on the page scroll away to make room for the new addition. Jessup flips through the dog-eared ricepaper pages to the essay "Papa and His Time" by Prof. E.C. Gwaltney, Ph.D. Jessup's margin notes and underlinings from college are still barely legible as faded pencil graffiti. Then there it is, appearing in a newly vacant part of the page: "after the publication of *The Old Man and the Sea*, a nearly flawless short novel, Hemingway was awarded the Pulitzer and Nobel prizes with a promptness but suggested an overdue recognition."

The anger bursts within him more explosively than last time, and Jessup flings the book at the shelves lining one wall of his cramped apartment.

"It's mine!" he cries for the thousandth time. "Fucking *damn* it!" He stares at his word processor's glowing screen…

---*Great Works of Western Literature*, Mark Bourne, F&SF, Sept. 1994, p. 7.

< change event focused, combined with stress in the present >

7 of 16

"I'm going to change into my overalls now," I said, heading for the bedroom.

When you're married to a god, you have to watch what you say.

"What an intriguing idea," he said. He pointed at me.

The next instant I lay on the ground, flatter than I was comfortable being, without the power of vision, and incapable of independent motion. My sense of touch had changed. I was aware of myself as a multitude of threads interwoven, with acres of thready skin.

When he picked me up and put me on, I sensed him as a series of textures and varying temperatures, moisture differences and body oils and sweat, skin and hair and heat...

---*Salvage Efforts*, Nina Kiriki Hoffman, F&SF, Aug. 1999, p. 120.

< change event focused, social stress in present >

8 of 16

It's amazing how life can change in the space of the day, an hour, a minute. That's a fact of my business. *Gossip Hourly* specializes in change --sometimes even initiates it.

But I didn't expect the changes that came after Detective Frank Forino's last official visit to my office. When he barged in, I thought the entire interaction was going to be routine.

He came through the doors unannounced -- somehow he scared my receptionist -- carrying a palmtop as thin as a piece of paper, and before I could decide whether I wanted to greet him or throw him out, he thrust the tiny screen at me.

"Looks like one of yours," he said...

---*Flowers and the Last Hurrah,* Kristine Kathryn Rusch, Analog, March 1999, p. 52.

< backfill combined with disaster, foreshadowed >

9 of 16

The morning of the raid I sat in a stolen minivan at the intersection of Game Farm Road and Alice Hollow Road, listening to a professional killer talk about compost. The killer's name was Ed. He was a skinny old guy with a big puff of hair and beard covering his whole head. Rumor had it that he had killed at least 11 men -- loggers and timber executives out in Oregon and northern California. He certainly did know a lot about organic farming…

---*The Alien Abduction,* James L. Cambias, F&SF, Sept. 2000, p. 4.

< backfill combined with violence foreshadowed >

10 of 16

The tested me again and again to ensure that the implant had properly salvaged the functions of damaged tissues. "An experimental procedure," a doctor said once, actually volunteering information. I had learned to hoard my questions. In return they accepted it and I chose not to say if I felt any pain here, or here, or here; if I remember. Perhaps they thought I no longer understood pain, or my past. They were right on one count…

---*Echoes Down an Endless Hall,* Yoon Ha Lee, F&SF, Apr. 2000, p. 117.

< Spec-oddity combined with Social Stress and suffering, past and present >

11 of 16

FROM A COSMOLOGICAL perspective, the sun was a solitary, isolated on the fringes of its galaxy. The supergiant belonged in spectral class K5. Seen more closely, it appeared as a dull smoky globe, a candle about to gutter out, the smoke consisting of myriads of particles dancing in the solar magnetism.

Despite its size, it was a cold thing, registering no more than 3600K. All about its girth, stretching far out along the plane of the eclectic, a series of artificial spheres moved in attendance. Each of these spheres contained captive solar systems.

The species which brought the globes here over vast distances called themselves the...

---*Steppenpferd,* Brian W. Aldiss, F&SF, Feb. 2000, p. 149.

< backfill >

12 of 16

When the shadows started appearing -- when things and people who had never even been before started appearing -- no one knew quite what to make of them. You and I didn't, I who in large part was responsible for exhuming them. When strangers and the dead began to flash through our homes and public places, ghost tales abounded. I, trying to be a scientist, sought to understand. I was fiercely unwilling to accept that these floating visions of bases were ghosts. Especially when my Laura showed up…

---*Circles of Light and Shadow,* Christopher McKitterick, Analog, Feb. 1999, p. 112.

< backfill >

13 of 16

He and the dog sneezed simultaneously.

"God bless," muttered the dog.

Ridge Gilby took a step back from the workbench. "Hey, my dogbots aren't supposed to sneeze," he said, frowning.

The large chrome-plated robot dog was lying on its side, the panel in its midsection dangling open to allow access to the inner circuitry. "Well, that's one of the reasons Mr. Dannenberg returned me for this free overhaul."

Rubbing the plaz handle of the electrodescrewer across his slightly plump chin, Gilby said, "It might be better, too, Rex, if you got that snide tone out of your voice."...

---*My Pal Clunky,* Ron Goulart, Analog, June 1998, p. 102.

< Spec-oddity, unclassified >

14 of 16

I said to my friend, George, over a beer recently (his beer; I was having a ginger ale), "How's your implet doing these days?"

George claims he has a two-centimeter-tall demon at his beck and call. I can never get him to admit he's lying. Neither can anyone else.

He glared at me balefully, then said, "Oh, yes, you're the one who knows about it! I hope you haven't told anyone else!"

"Not a word," I said. "It's quite sufficient that I think you're crazy. I don't need anyone thinking the same of me." (Besides, he has told at least half a dozen people about the demon, to my personal knowledge, so there's no necessity of *my* being indiscreet.)...

---*The Smile That Loses,* Isaac Asimov, F&SF, Nov. 1982, p. 70.

< Spec-oddity with Social Stress in the present, combined with Curiosity >

15 of 16

"But what if I don't want to live forever?"

Schrader looked at his wife and frowned. *Agnes, don't be so difficult!*

Swiveling a little in her chair behind the long wooden desk, Dr. Renard replied calmly, "The treatment won't make you immortal. It makes you much more resistant to infections and life-threatening diseases, but you'll be just as vulnerable to accidental injuries. And, of course, it makes you younger."...

---*The Best is Yet to Be*, Analog, Feb. 1989, p. 86. < Spec-oddity in a dialogue opening, Social Stress in the present >

16 of 16

"There are sentients on the third planet."

Ch'klorb, captain of the starship *Omnivore*, rolled glumly across the floor of the cargo bay. The Prime Mover studied the two objects Cailar had asked it here to see, then vibrated, "I think you're reading too much into this junk."

The ship's chaplain bowed his head solemnly. "I humbly disagree, Your Roundness. As I just explained, based on how they're constructed and where we found them, I'm convinced they're space probes produced by a Rating-10 civilization. I was an engineer before joining the priesthood, and recognize what functions several parts of them served...

---*Achromamorph's Burden,* H.G. Stratmann, Analog, Feb. 2000, p.32.

<Spec-oddity, combined with conflict in the present >

CATALOG D

Curiosity

1 of 4

I like to believe that I began life as someone else.

But life has gradually remade me, as it does all of us. Reshaping my matrix. Remolding my pliable soul. Transforming my nature with minuscule touches and the rare little leap, improving as well as degrading those vital and subtle and basically immeasurable qualities that very much define what is me.

This happened to a stranger some 30 years ago.

He was brilliant and cocky -- an extraordinarily loud undergraduate. A bad mix of traits, that. Give the prick any excuse, and he used to sing his own praises, and telling everyone in earshot that here posed the full-blown genius. An intellectual titan. The lighthouse shining through across ignorant black seas. With embarrassing ease, he predicted great things for himself and anyone standing in his shadow. Proof of his brilliance was everywhere. His IQ scores. His easy good grades. The trademark audacity wearing its useful veneer of boyish charm. Plus a certain knack for impressing his otherwise tired and dispirited white-haired professors.

Thirty years ago, this happened to me.

I was that bright abrasive prick. And my school was a little university that frankly lacked the prestige and professional heavyweights found in the best schools. Steering back across three increasingly fogbound decades, trying to resurrect how I got to be where I was, I'm sure that I never gave Harvard or Stanford or MIT any real chance to claim me. And why? Because I secretly understood that I was nothing but a smart young man. Talented, but only to a point. Genius would see through my bluster, and the only way I could feel like the giant was to remain in a smaller, tamer pond.

I was an insufferable, incandescent pain in the ass.

And still am, if you happen to be listening to certain colleagues or lost friends or any of my several ex-wives…

---*The Gulf*, Robert Reed, F&SF, Oct./Nov. 2000, p. 112.

2 of 4

The Navigators towered over the desert. Unmoving, enigmatic, ominous, they thrust ribbed bowls at the sky and. *Help us.* Moonlight filled the bowls, silvered the supporting beams and struts, and touched the network of ground rails that connected the giants with each other.

They shall be a sign of my promise to you.

Hammond hunched forward on his horse. The wind was warm and dry out of the north. The breath of the Almighty. He lowered his binoculars, unslung them, and handed them to James. "God is good," he said.

The old man lowered his cowl. "Amen."

There were eighty-three of them, of identical dimensions, each approximately ten stories high from its wheeled base to the highest point on the bowl. Most of the

Navigators pointed in the same direction, toward the southwest, at an elevation of about thirty-two degrees. A few, out of step, looked elsewhere, two or three toward Ayer's rock, others away to the east, one toward Hammond as if it were contemplating *him.* Several had collapsed into the dry earth.

Iris Windrider is gone to look for Eden. The Navigators showed her the way, as they shall one day show the way for you.

"There was a time when we sailed the twilight," said James, chanting the line.

Hammond responded: *"And the greatest of those who rode the wind was Iris."*

Hammond turned in his saddle. "It's always good to come here," he said.

The old man sighed and handed the glasses back. "It is. And maybe tonight the old promise will be fulfilled." The wind pulled at his white hair.

"God in his own good time," said Hammond. In James's presence, he always felt a rush of piety.

And when the sun grew deadly, Iris fled beyond the sea, to find a green, cool land.

James frowned. "I would *like* to believe," he said, wearily. "I really would. But I will admit to you, George, and deny it if you quote me: I suspect there was no

Iris, and there is no land but this." He shook off the mood that was visibly settling on him. "God forgive me."

" But they have *moved*, James. Surely, the promise is about to be fulfilled."

The older man allowed his mount to move slowly forward, across sand and crabgrass. "In my lifetime? I would give much to see it, George. But there have been reports before." The moon was cool and soft in a clear sky. "The Faithful tend to see what they hope to see."

The giants stood silent…

---*Windrider,* Jack McDevitt, Asimov's, July 1994, p. 112.

3 of 4

I'M SARAH BRADY. YES *THAT* SARAH BRADY. I was production manager for the second coming of Jesus Christ, and I can tell you it wasn't easy. Here on the Moon, of course, nothing is easy. And on the Moon or not, nothing involving my crazy husband could ever be easy at all.

By now, most people have seen interiors of his Warp Experiment Lab, and know what it looked like. Just a typical ordinary Moon base laboratory, that's where Matthew worked. Gauges, monitors, power fibers and the rest. Actually, the real boss was old Professor Peabody up on her control dais, high above the giant metallic knot of toroids that she herself had designed. Beside her at the banks of instruments were the researchers: Frederic, Teresa, Krishnan, and that overgrown schoolboy, Mathew Brady, Ph.D. It was all his fault. I know it was.

Who else would have tried running the last work cycle on maximum power just for a special Christmas treat?

Who else but Mathew Brady?...

---*When Jesus Came to the Moon for Christmas*, David Redd, F&SF, Jan. 1991, p. 138.

4 of 4

Human beings called me Mustardseed. As satellites of Uranus go, I wasn't much -- barely three kilometers in radius compared to Titania's five hundred or so. I wasn't even in the same plane as Uranus' other moons -- I sat way out here in the plane of the ecliptic, watching the rest of them roll around the solar system with their poles where the equator's of proper planets belong. Not that I was much of a solar system conformist either; oh, no, I orbited Uranus the wrong way around with my angular momentum vector bass ackward. The rock different, that was me. Why, it's almost as if I had a mind of my own even back when the solar system was formed!

But that came along some four and a half billion years later, about thirty million years ago -- only yesterday as the stars reckon things.

It took human beings long enough to notice me. Well, I'll excuse the first thirty million years or so because they weren't really human beings. But you would have thought that by the time their probes went whizzing by here like bullets from the inner solar system hell and they'd built telescopes on their own overstuffed Moon that were nearly as wide across as I was, someone would have noticed…

---*Mustardseed,* G. David Nordley, Asimov's, Sept. 1999, p. 100.

Exercise

Exercises can be pretty hit-or-miss, but I include this because it might be helpful. The idea of recopying another author's work word-for-word, seems like a waste of time. Yet a number of authors, David Brin included, recommend it. I've read of authors who've recopied entire novels (!). It seems illogical that mere copying could affect one's creativity. But I wonder - could this objection, in itself, be irrational? Even Ayn Rand, the goddess of "logic," admitted that much of the writing process was unconscious — was a matter of feeding the right question(s) to her subconscious. By analogy, if I'm interested in being a Running Back in football, is it going to hurt me to mimic, say, Tony Dorsett's running style just to see what happens? At the very least it will build strength. The fact is, we really don't know how the subconscious of any particular writer "works." But I can argue that recopying may encode certain "professional" patterns into the subconscious for later use.

That said, here's the exercise: choose a hook from the catalogs above. Recopy it word-for-word. Then substitute your own nouns and verbs. Not to use in a real story, but to get a feel-for that kind of opening. Here's an example of a Stress / Social Stress opening taken from *The New Yorker:*

> "Hooey," Mr. Oamaru says, working his fork with silly urgency. A single pea is caught between his square front teeth. "That boy Rangi can sing. The boy just needs a friend is all. You be that, Tek. You be that friend."
>
> My mother's prim smile confirms that I should be that friend…
>
> ---*Accident Brief,* Karen Russell, The New Yorker, issue 2006-06-19; Posted 2006-06-12.

Rewrite:

> "Yeppers," Coach says, stirring his stew with hulking vigor. Beef strands cling to his front teeth. "That boy Chang can play football. The boy just needs a friend. That's all. You be that, Jerry. That's an order. You be that friend."
>
> My mother's delighted smile confirms that I should, indeed, be that friend…

A FEW FINAL NOTES

- Avoid "repeatitis." Readers intensely dislike reading the same word in too-close proximity to itself.

- Avoid metaphors until your characters and setting are well-established in the reader's mind. In all of the 1,400 short fiction openings I examined, only two or three used a metaphor in the first paragraph, and only when the context was crystal clear.

- I'm indebted to David Brin for pointing out the importance of deciding on the correct Point of View for your story. POV trumps the opening in importance, since it applies to how well the entire story will work. If you get the feeling that your story just isn't working, take a look at POV. One of the best books on the subject is Character and Viewpoint by Orson Scott Card.

TESTING YOUR OPENING

The opening is the first thing an editor will see, which is why a couple of the Hatrack River Writing Workshop forums are extremely helpful. For short fiction, the "Fragments and Feedback for Short Works" forum or for longer works, "Fragments and Feedback for Novels" forum are great tools. You can post the first 13 lines of your story and get detailed feedback within 24 hours. Hatrack River is also free.

Other workshops, such as Critters.org, will of course look at your entire story.

Do be aware that while Critters.org stresses diplomacy, critiques on Hatrack River may be extremely blunt. In response to a member comment, "I remembered that the whole point is to try to improve the selection based on the comments!", Hatrack River administrator Kathleen Dalton-Woodbury had this to say:

> Not exactly. I'd say that the point is more to consider what the comments have to say about the selection and decide if any of the comments are relevant to what you are trying to accomplish as a writer with the story. If any of the comments are relevant, then you consider how to use

> what they tell you to get the story closer to what you want it to be.
>
> Yes, improving the selection is important, but the comments are only comments, only opinions, only reactions. You are the author, and you should only pay attention to two kinds of comments:
>
> 1) those that resonate with what you are trying to do and get you excited to write more
>
> 2) those expressed by three of more critiquers on the same problem, and even then, what they suggest may not be the answer. Instead, all those comments do is point you at a problem you need to think about more.

Always remember that, no matter what, critiques are only the opinions and reactions of that one reader.

AFTERWORD

I hope all of you who feel like your openings need improvement can benefit from this monograph. If you do find it helpful, I'd appreciate "Before" versions of your stories and then "After" versions. Please send them or any feedback to:

rlqualkinbush@hotmail.com

Thanks, and Best Wishes,

Robert Qualkinbush,
Cross Junction, Virginia

ReAnimus Press

Breathing Life into Great Books

If you enjoyed this book we hope you'll tell others or write a review! We also invite you to subscribe to our newsletter to learn about our new releases and join our affiliate program (where you earn 12% of sales you recommend) at www.ReAnimus.com.

Here are more ebooks you'll enjoy from ReAnimus Press, available from ReAnimus Press's web site, Amazon.com, bn.com, etc.:

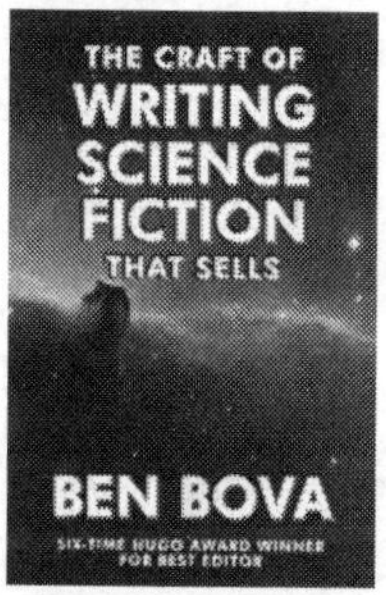

The Craft of Writing Science Fiction that Sells, by Ben Bova

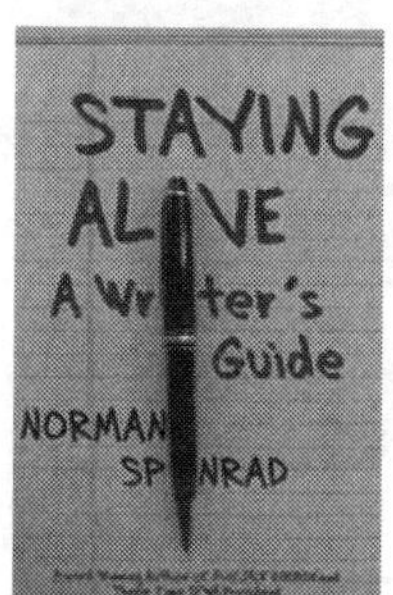

Staying Alive - A Writer's Guide, by Norman Spinrad

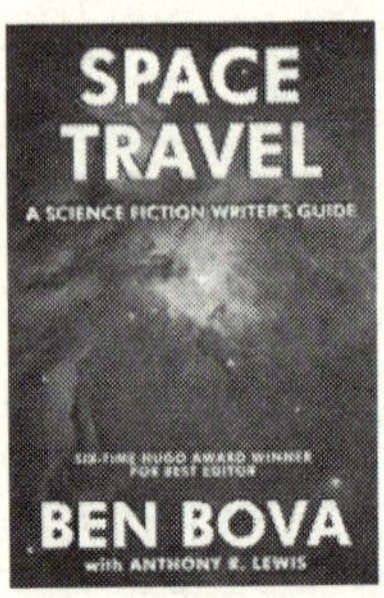

Space Travel—A Guide for Writers,
by Ben Bova

Experiment Perilous: The 'Bug Jack Barron' Papers, an essay for writers by Norman Spinrad

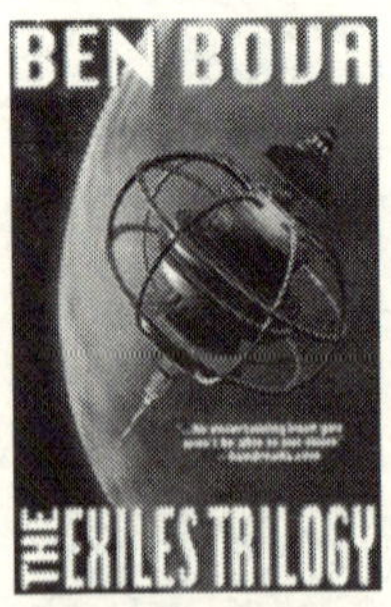

The Exiles Trilogy, by Ben Bova

The Star Conquerors, by Ben Bova
(Standard Edition and
Special Collector's Edition)

Test of Fire, by Ben Bova

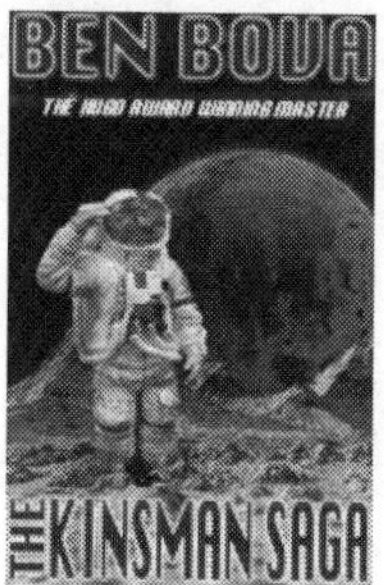

The Kinsman Saga, by Ben Bova

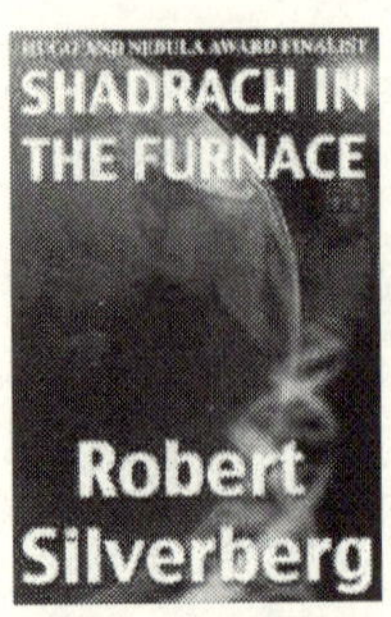

Shadrach in the Furnace, by Robert Silverberg

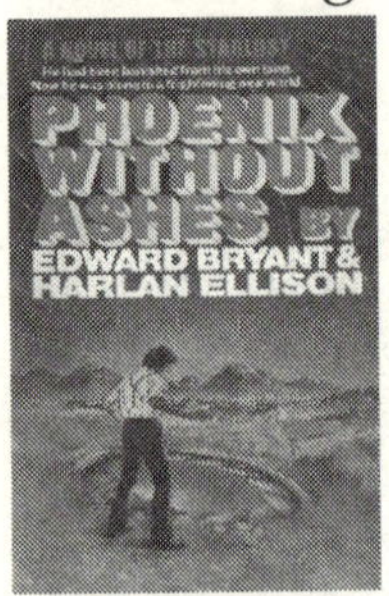

Phoenix Without Ashes,
by Harlan Ellison and Edward Bryant

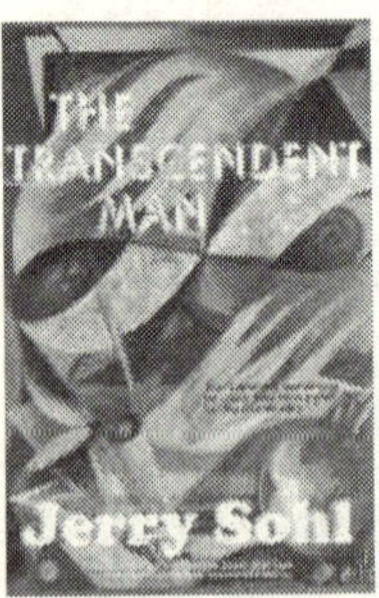

The Transcendent Man, by Jerry Sohl

Night Slaves, by Jerry Sohl

Bloom, by Wil McCarthy

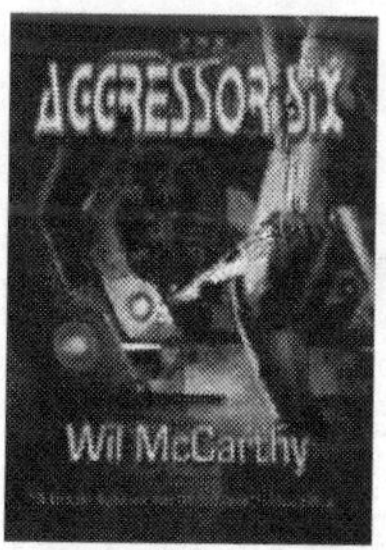

Aggressor Six, by Wil McCarthy

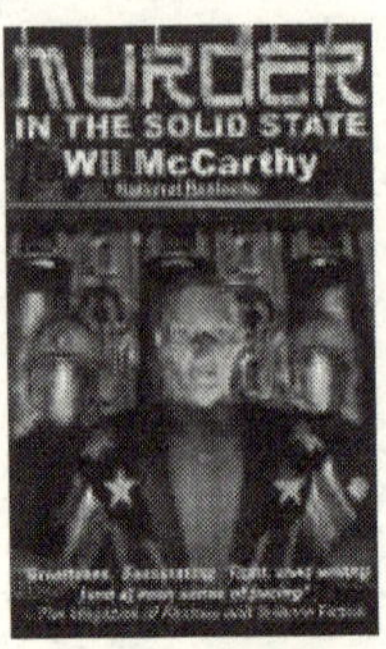

Murder in the Solid State,
by Wil McCarthy

Flies from the Amber, by Wil McCarthy

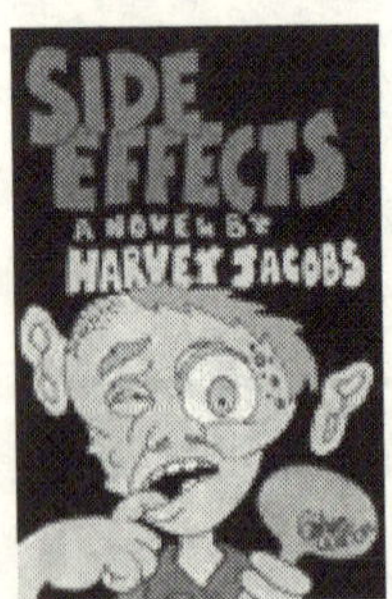

Side Effects, by Harvey Jacobs

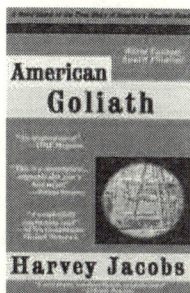

Coming soon:

Futureproofing Your Writing: How to avoid anachronisms in fiction to keep your prose timeless, by Andrew Burt

Improving relationships in Speculative Fiction (Or Shhh! How I caught a glimpse of The Secret of great fiction), by Andrew Burt

Watch for these and many more great titles from ReAnimus Press!

Made in the USA
Charleston, SC
12 May 2015